# Living by the
# Point of My Spear

A study of the Life of Muhammad
and his Personality
## Zaki Ameen

### (Ramsees the third)

Living by the point of my spear is one of Muhammad's
sayings - sahih Al Bukhari, Chapter Jihad and Biography,
saying 2913 and Musssnad Al Imam Ahammed saying 5409
and 4869.

Felibri.com

# About the Author

Zaki Ameen dedicated his life to Islam. He was raised as a Muslim and studied for a degree in Sharia law, in order to become a qualified Imam. Zaki earned his living from preaching and teaching the principles of Islam, working as an Imam in Egypt, Iraq, Yemen and many gulf states.

In the course of his career as an Imam, he started to realise how the teaching of Muhammad and the Quran were used to deceive followers, in order to gain control, money and power. It was with deep agony that he realised what a fool he had been and how he had been brainwashed by a system that had been refined over centuries and how he had, in turn, brainwashed others.

Zaki left Islam and the Mosques and emigrated to the United States, to start a new career and a new life. He became a tax payer making a positive contribution to society. He now saw that being an Imam was like being a parasite, spreading lies and encouraging others to spread the lies of Muhammad.

Zaki started to accept, respect and love people as they are, without prejudice. He accepted all people as equals, including Muslims, whether they obeyed the orders of Allah, or not. This was a genuine love he had never felt before, unfettered by doctrine or religion.

What happened on 9/11 shocked him to his core and it was shortly after that that he realised he could not simply stop following Muhammad, but he had to do more. He became obsessed and haunted by an irresistible urge to let the world know what he had discovered about Muhammad and Islam.

Thus began the journey to write a true biography of Muhammad and the true story of Islam – a long and dangerous journey to write, translate and publish the book that became *Living by the Point of My Spear.*

# Introduction

*iving by the point of my spear* is addressed and dedicated primarily to Arabs and Muslims, however all readers will find content that is interesting, well researched and informative.

*Living by the point of my spear* analyses Muhammad's character and is a published account of his real biography and other facts that have disappeared from Arabic literature for 1,400 years.

It is an uncompromised and uncompromising account, showing the dark side of Muhammad and Islam, without any consideration or fear of the swords, prisons or torture by Muslim clergymen and governors.

This book is free from any influence of western governments or western intellectuals – whether they are Christian, Jewish, atheist or Marxist, regardless of whether they are right or wrong.

*Living by the point of my spear* is not just a collection of philosophical contemplations and theories, it originates from the agonies, struggles and disappointments of Muslims. It is change from within.

This book is based solely on Arabic literature and references and its author is an Arab and former Imam of a mosque, who understands the Arabic mentality and the suffering of Muslims as individuals and as a society. It is the first time ever that an Arab has spoken out with such honesty and clarity on the secret truth of Muhammad and Islam and is written from an Arabic / Islamic point of view.

*Living by the point of my spear* was originally written in Arabic in seven chapters and the most important chapter, The Secret of Islam's Longevity, has been translated into English and published here with some important extracts from other chapters at the end of this book.

Civilisation evolves and develops as time passes, values and ethics for the entire planet, not just 'western civilisation', are an essential part of this process and of the maturation of humanity. Around the globe people of all religions and creeds are willing to defend the values of human rights, the human freedoms of thought and speech, democracy and the rights of women.

'Western civilisation' and, in fact, any civilisation, must never kneel to the primitive tools of many Islamic groups who use violence and terror to further their aims. This inevitably will eventually destabilise the very basis of Islam itself.

It is essential that the truth behind the dogma of fundamentalist Islamic thought is illuminated. Light must be shed on the deceits, fabrications and misguidance of many Islamic scholars, theorists, historians and so called 'holy' men.

The time is right for this book, this gift of mine to the world at large and the people of all civilisations and religions.

# Table of Contents

## The Secret of Islam's Longevity

*I* hope to convince you that Islam is nothing more than Bedouin customs and traditions, transformed by Muhammad and his followers into a divine religion and doctrine. What then is the secret behind Islam's longevity?

In order to answer this question, we must understand all the circumstances and changes that have helped Islam to continue.

I will answer this question objectively with all the resources I have available. I will be accused of racism, chauvinism and of stirring up animosity, but none of these accusations move me. I am only driven by arriving at the entire truth in as direct a fashion as possible.

These are the reasons and factors that have helped Islam to endure for so long:

### Muhammad's Double Standards

Muhammad grew up in difficult circumstances, working as a shepherd and struggling with his love/hate relationship and his loyalties towards his Quraish tribe. The reality of an oppressed shepherd's life was the cornerstone of his thinking and the mainstay of his consciousness.

The Hadiths on jinn (the ghosts), his contempt for dogs and donkeys, and his preference for camels, sheep, and roosters – all these point clearly to the mentality of a shepherd. (All of these sayings are written and fully explained and supported in an earlier chapter of the book).

After Muhammad married Khadija, he became rich and left the pastoral life, however his nickname Abu Kabsha[1] stuck to him like glue. He would have paid any price to get rid of this label!

Muhammad's grandfather, Abdul Mutlib, was one of the senior Hanif. He infused Hanif teaching and thinking via Muhammad's uncle Abu Talib throughout Muhammad's home. This teaching exposed Muhammad to the thinking and teaching that the Hanifs took from Judaism, Christianity, Zoroastrianism and the Sabians of Yemen. In addition, Muhammad increased this exposure by travelling to the region of Syria and the Yemen.

The doctrine and teaching of Hanif included the art of concealing and manipulating facts in order to look better and achieve one's goals. This gave Muhammad a cover for his own fake stories, exaggeration of facts and outright lies. Muhammad learned these principles and ways during his childhood from his uncle Abu Talib. He lived in a culture of exaggeration and misrepresentation that went along with the misery, poverty, and oppression of a shepherd's life.

As a result of Muhammad's upbringing, he developed a unique personality, a greater understanding of Bedouin

---

[1] This nickname was the feminized version of 'little sheep'. It was a constant reminder that before he claimed to be a prophet, he was merely a shepherd. Sahih Al Bukhari , Alwahi (7)

Hanif is a Hebrew term meaning to conceal, to pretend, to lie, Anwar hekmat, Women and Quran p29. Later this term was used by Muhammad to the followers of Abraham, who was a hanif Muslim.

society and the ability to converse with the various classes according to their understanding and needs. This became clear in his manner of speech in the early Hadiths to the leaders and nobles and his Hadiths to the majority of his followers, the oppressed classes, such as the shepherds and slaves. There is a marked contrast between these Hadiths and sayings. He had a clear understanding of the needs and ambitions of these different classes.

(All these sayings are fully explained and supported in earlier chapters of the book).

Muhammad conveyed his expertise and understanding of different classes and how to manipulate them to other Muslim fellows, so much so that they became professionals in changing and fabricating facts and in anticipating and preparing for future developments. The caliphs following Muhammad, especially Abu Bakr and Omar, lived with Muhammad for over twenty years and learned these techniques well. They knew that Muhammad wasn't a prophet, but learned the skill of fabrication and revision at his feet. They, in turn, taught their followers, the 'religious men,' who have continued this chain of lies and perversion to the present day.

Muhammad was highly sophisticated in establishing his religion based on lies which required the deletion of important historical facts and the fabrication of an alternate history in their place. As a result, it is extremely difficult to refute this religion without knowledge of Muhammad, his upbringing, and the people and events that played a large part in the establishment of this religion.

Muhammad relied on a few fundamentals when establishing his religion, such as:

## Manipulation of the Quran

The Quran is a diary of Muhammad, a register of this era's incidents, what others said and how Muhammad responded.

The Meccan verses in the Quran that were revealed and written during the first ten years of Muhammad's prophetic calling were included among the Medina verses in the last thirteen years of his life. Their inclusion and the manner of their inclusion increases the level of obscurity and complexity in understanding this religion and makes the chain of events far harder to follow.

The number of Medinan verses which Muhammad inserted in each Meccan chapter are listed below.

| Chapter | Total verses | Number of verses written in Medina |
|---------|-------------|-------------------------------------|
| Sura al-An'am | 165 verses | 6 |
| Sura al-Ar'af | 205 verses | 5 |
| Sura Yunis | 106 verses | 2 |
| Sura al-Nahal | 128 verses | 1 |
| Sura al-Asr | 110 verses | 8 |
| Sura Maryam | 98 verses | 3 |
| Sura al-Qasas | 87 verses | 5 |

Likewise, Muhammad inserted Meccan verses into Medinan suras, such as the sura al-Anfal, which contains 7 verses written in Mecca.

Ibn Kathir states in his commentary on the Quran that if Muhammad received revelation, he used to say 'place these verses in the chapters that mention such and such.' If he then received a new revelation, he said, 'Place these verses in the chapter that mentions such and such.'[2]

In other words, Muhammad was continually manipulating the Quran and changing the places of verses. In front of one group of scribes he gave specific verses, in front of another group of scribes he recited different verses and placed them in other suras so that each of Muhammad's scribes had a Quran that differed from the others. It appears that he did this in order to obscure the chain of events so that the historical events in these chapters and verses could not be easily understood.

---

[2] Ibn Kathir, pg. 859.

## The Abrograotor and the Abrogated:
## How Muhammad rewrote the Quran.

*M*uhammad was a politician, ambitious for power, money and domination over the Qureish and the Arabs. He began his Hanif mission peacefully with his call to worship Allah. In his Meccan verses, he used amicable discourse to cause people to fear the punishments of Allah. After this calling failed, Muhammad's strategy changed to violence, turning into the leader of an armed mafia, bent on cutting off roads, looting, and robbery, all done under the pretext of spreading a new religion. Because of this change in approach, Muhammad had to change the Quran.

Muhammad invented a new celestial term, which he called 'abrogation' (*naskh*). It equates to 'deletion'. This means that Allah changed his mind on what he had said earlier in the Quran. In fact, it was a convenient method for Muhammad to adjust the Quran to the needs of the moment. For instance, Muhammad alleged in his Quran that Allah would rain down severe punishment on anyone who shed blood in the Kaaba and that Allah would send special birds to shoot fiery rocks against any who did so. However,

Muhammad then said that Allah, 'the Best of Planners,'[3] had changed his mind and allowed Muhammad and his army past the velvet rope so they could kill and slaughter his political opponents. After that, another revelation just in, Mecca was off limits to everyone after Muhammad and his army entered the Kaaba.

The majority of Muhammad's Quran was just a record of daily events involving Muhammad, along with the sayings of others. As time passed these events and sayings lost their importance, so Muhammad tried to get rid of these chapters and verses by saying that Allah had abrogated and cancelled them. In addition, Muhammad's many sexual escapades and dalliances meant a constant need for revelation to 'clean things up.' His marriage to his adopted son's wife and the need to justify the changes in his mood and disposition, as his current urges dictated, forced him to come up with the recurring use of the ghost Jibreel (According to Muhammad, Jibreel was a white ghost who gave him revelations. More information about Jibreel follows later in this chapter).

Ibn Masoud, one of Muhammad's scribes, said, 'Muhammad gave me a verse, and I wrote it down in my volume. Later that night when I went to bed, I couldn't remember anything that I had written. When I returned to the volume to check it, I found that the sheet was blank. I informed Muhammad, and he said "take it easy, Ibn Masoud, They were lifted and cancelled yesterday."[4] Ibn

---

[3] The Arabic term '*maker*' means, 'to deceive, delude, cheat, etc.' Muhammad repeatedly used the comparative form of this term to show that Allah is more devious than any other. He presents the term as an admirable attribute, but is secretly laughing at the Muslims for gullibly accepting this term. English translations use the term 'plotter' for men, but soften this term to 'planner' for Allah. See Sura 8, *Anfal,* verse 30, Yusuf Ali translation.

[4] Systematic Readings in Islam, pg. 197. The text is quoted from 'The Abrogator and the Abrogated' by Ibn Salameh, pg.5 (1960 Printing).

Masoud was one of the devoted servants of Muhammad; he was responsible for Muhammad's shoes.

Ibn Masoud, a killer and thug, feigned the acts and sayings of a holy man to get the Bedouin to believe him, even to the point of believing Muhammad's account when Allah sent Jibreel the ghost to erase and remove divinely inspired text. In this story, we see that Allah, the 'Best of Planners' changed his mind and decided to remove this verse. Therefore, the 'Best of Planners' decided to send a revelation to scrap the text from Ibn Masoud's volume. Muhammad must have been inwardly laughing at his followers and the Bedouins' gullibility to believe his religion and that the 'Best of Planners' would change his mind and justify these acts to suit one man.

Muhammad said in his Quran 'Allah erases as he pleases and confirms as he pleases. He has the mother book.'[5] Muhammad spoke of the mother book in another Hadith, saying that the 'Best of Planners' had written down every event, both heavenly and earthly, throughout the course of history for every people, nation and individual, establishing all the conditions of creation up to the moment. Indeed, according to Muhammad, this book - *Living by the point of my spear* - is written and established in the mother book. However, with all this, the 'Best of Planners' changed his mind and erased as he pleased and established as he pleased.

Muhammad explained these constant changes as a test or ordeal from Allah – to separate the true Muslims from those who are not. It is clear that the real reason for the abrogation (or deletion) was the change in Muhammad's political position.

Muhammad abrogated and changed so many verses that this put later religious scholars in a state of total confusion. In the sura al-Baqarah, for example, the scholars have failed

---

[5] Quran, sura 13, Al-Ra'ad, the Thunder, verse 39.

miserably to solve or explain, no matter how absurdly, the problem Muhammad put them in with this verse. Verse 234 of the sura al-Baqarah states 'And if any of you die and leave widows behind, they shall wait concerning themselves four months and ten days.' This abrogated and deleted the verse that comes directly after it! Verse 240 from the same chapter states: 'Those of you who die and leave widows should bequeath for their widows a year's maintenance and residence.'[6]

To explain these verses, before Islam, a widow could stay in her deceased husband's house for a full year after his death. The sons of the deceased husband or his family were responsible for paying the costs for this year, after which the women had the right to remarry. Since Islam is an extension of Bedouin values and customs, Muhammad received by revelation text to this effect, as stated in verse 240 above. After that, he noticed that the costs for a whole year were significant and that women were undeserving of such expenses according to this Bedouin custom. The new rule in Muhammad's Quran was that the widow could remain in her deceased husband's home for only four months and ten days, with no cost of living allowance and get a fourth of the inheritance. Through the exaggerated use of abrogation and changing the location of verses, Muhammad placed the new ruling earlier in the sura Baqarah and the old Bedouin law later in the same sura.

Imagine how this would look to you today. What if a judicial body issued a ruling on some matter. The ruling went into fine detail to explain the decision, and included a paragraph at the end of all the details stating that there will be a future ruling from the same judicial body on this same subject that will conflict with this present ruling, so please pay no attention to this future ruling when it comes. How would that feel to you?

---

[6] Ibn Kathir, pg. 299-300.

When faced with this conflict, Muslim scholars decided to accept the highly questionable interpretation that the first verse abrogated and cancelled the second verse. Muslims could have easily interpreted this differently and drawn the opposite conclusion.

Why did Muhammad change the location of verses and insert Medinan verses in Meccan chapters and vice versa? We can see the cunning of this man, the same cunning that he attributes to Allah, when we examine his spectacular night flight on his winged horse Buraq from Mecca to Jerusalem and his return to Mecca the same night. This verse was recorded in Meccan chapters, even with the precise detail that he started his amazing journey in Mecca and returned there, but what was the real reason for it being in a Meccan chapter and not a Medinan chapter?

The difference was to cover the historical fact that the story of the flight occurred after Muhammad heard the same story from Salman al-Farisi, when Muhammad was in Medina. Muhammad plagiarized the story and inserted it among the Meccan verses to cut off any future enquiry that might arrive at the truth.

Aisha exposed these lies and said that Muhammad never left the bed[7] on the night that he said he flew on his winged horse to Jerusalem. This is further proof that it occurred in Medina after his marriage to Aisha.

Aisha gave this testimony for two reasons: first, to expose Muhammad and to establish that this strange journey occurred in Medina after Muhammad came to know Salman al-Farisi and then placed this story in Meccan chapters. Secondly, she wanted to refute the idea that there was any flight. Muhammad did not fly. There was no winged horse. This story was only the figment of Muhammad's imagination.

---

[7] Sirat Rasul (Ibn Ishaq) p 309.

Muhammad took advantage of his Allah-given ability to change the location of verses to efface important historical facts and obscure any follow-up to Muhammad and his religion. After the Battle against Thakeef tribe in Al-Taf twon, where Muhammad's armies failed to enter the town despite a siege of the town for forty days, the rulers of Thakeef forced Muhammad to praise their pagan god Al-Lat the female deity and mention her favorably in his Quran. They actually forced Muhammad to magnify Al-Lat in his Quran.

He said in his Quran, in what is known as the Satanic Verses: the three pagan goddesses are highly respectful deities and their invocation, supplication (and not invitation as some Muslim exegetes translate) is the duty of all Muslims. Her adoration was expected to encourage the Muslim and non-Muslim Bedouins to visit the temple of Al-Lat in Al-Taf town and thus raise the income and profits of the townspeople, according to the conditions set by the delegation from Al-Taf during negotiations. With these verses, Muhammad's army entered Al-Taf without fighting while the people of Thakeef tribe remained pagan and paid the jizya (the high tax) to Muhammad. After a while, Muhammad moved the verses given in Medina and inserted them in the Meccan chapters as a pre-emptive disclaimer for the future.

Muhammad did not limit his manipulations and changes just to the Quran. His Hadiths contain bigger and more numerous contradictions than the Quran on wars and raids to square with Muhammad's need for military power and fighters to help him in these continuous wars.

Muhammad enticed the Bedouins with money, women, jewels and slaves. He encouraged and sanctioned temporary marriage, rape of captive wives, anal intercourse, ejaculation inside the vagina and vaginal penetration of captive women. (Again, earlier chapters cover this in more detail).

In other words, to do whatever they wanted. The important thing was to include his armies and fighters.

After the battle, Muhammad would return to the mosque and call for reform, crying and weeping, forbidding what he had just encouraged the previous day.

When preparing for a coming raid, Muhammad would then return to encouraging exactly what he had forbidden just a few days prior. These massive contradictions are found in the Hadiths of Muhammad. The numerous Muslim sects each take what they find advantageous from the Hadiths and deny those that don't justify their position, such as temporary marriage and the division between the Shi'ite and Sunni over the legality of temporary whoredom.

In conclusion, we see that Muhammad, who claimed that Allah, the 'Best of Planners' had every event that ever would be written in the 'mother book', changed and deleted the texts of both the Quran and the Hadiths to suit his own, selfish ends.

## Who was Jibreel the ghost / inspiring angel?

uhammad claimed that Jibreel, the ghost or inspiring angel, was sent by Allah to erase divinely inspired text.

He said that the inspiring angel in their first meeting ordered him to read, saying "Read in the name of your Allah repeatedly for three times", but he refused to read[8].

Muhammad concluded by saying "then I awoke from my sleep".

This tells us that the inspiring angel, Jibreel occurred only in a dream. If Muhammad's first encounter with Jibreel was a dream, it follows that all his so called encounters with Jibreel were actually nothing more than dreams.

If all Muhammad's inspiration came from dreams, then it follows that the Quran, the clergymen and the bloody wars and the thousands of fatalities that occurred from these wars have all sprung from a dream!

---

[8] Ibn Hisham part 3/ Pg 180

The Muslim leaders and clergymen try to deny and hide the fact that the inspiring angel and the prophecy are simply based on a dream!

## How was Muhammad's Holiness created?

uhammad himself fabricated a collection of stories and tales about his own holiness. He encouraged his followers and Islamic clergymen to exaggerate his holiness, specifically with regard to his childhood and the way in which magicians, clergymen and priests acknowledged that this miracle boy would be the future messenger.

The stories that Muhammad fabricated included one claiming that he had had a surgical operation when he was a child, in which a devil object had been removed from his body. This story ended with the trees shading him wherever he walked.

How do Muhammad's own fabrications compare to other accounts from that time? Let us read what Haleema Al-Sa'diah, Muhammad's wet nurse, said: 'I went to Mecca with a group of women seeking livelihood by breastfeeding infants. The other women refused to breastfeed Muhammad when they knew that he was orphan. For this reason, I breastfed him; I swear that if I had found somebody else, I would not have taken him.' [9]

This raises the question of how these women were not able to recognize the sign of prophecy, as the clergymen and priests did. The surprising thing is that all the priests who recognized this sign, from Bahiri to Waraqa bin Nofal, and believed that Muhammad was the expected prophet, did not embrace Islam.

If Muhammad was the promised prophet since his childhood, why did he worship and pray at, and sacrifice a sheep to, the statue of Al-Uzza, a female pagan deity and daughter of Allah? Let us read the text written by Ibn Ishaq in Sirat Rasul[10]:

Muhammad said 'I came back from Al-Taf town and met Zaid Bin Amro, a senior Hanif, at a hill not far from Mecca. I had my lunch with me, which included pieces of sheep meat that were sacrificed before our statues; I offered some of it to Zaid saying: eat some of this food, uncle'. Zaid asked Muhammad: 'is this meat that which was sacrificed to your statues?' Muhammad replies: 'YES!' Zaid answered: 'I do not eat this meat, I do not need it.' Zaid then started to criticize the statues and their worshippers, including Muhammad, saying these statues did not benefit or harm anyone. The story concludes with Muhammad saying that after this incident he did not worship or sacrifice before a statue.

Muhammad promoted his allegation of being a prophet and increased his apparent holiness among the Bedouin by fabricating these stories and wearing Kohl (eye liner) twice a day. This illusion of holiness has increased exponentially to the present day, to the extent that you can no longer question the holiness of this so-called miracle man.

---

[9] Ibn Ishaq in Sirat Rasul P 100.
[10] Ibn Ishaq in Sirat Rasul P165.

For the real motives behind Muhammad's claims to prophecy, please see an extract from another chapter at the end of this book.

## Why the Quran is hard to understand and easily misused

When writing the Quran, Muhammad benefited greatly from knowing stories of Jewish prophets. Zaid Bin Thabit11 (3), a writer of The Quran, said: I was ordered by Muhammad to learn the Syriac language (a type of Aramaic language, the language of the Bible, the Syrians and Iraqi Christians) and Muhammad paid me for this and I became professional in this language. I used to write to Muhammad in this language and read to him their books.'

Muslim exegetes interpret 'their books' as their correspondence but the word book 'Katab' in Arabic means their holy book. This information clarifies how Muhammad knew about stories of Jewish prophets and the resemblance of prophets' stories in both the Quran and the Bible. Muhammad used to fill his Quran up with these stories by repetition and addition. He mentioned Moses 96 times in his Quran, however you might notice that these stories are added in the middle of verses without any introduction or cohesion. They appear and vanish suddenly in the same style, then will reappear again in later verses in the same chapter. The ordering of these stories indicates a loss of continuity, cohesion and sequence.

Muhammad frequently sent coded message to a specific person or tribe and then wrote of this communication in his Quran.

Muhammad used to monitor his Quran carefully. If he realized that his coded message to a specific body started to appear too clearly in a given chapter and the situation

---

[11] Al Seera Al Nabawiya (Al Halabiya) Khaffaji Al Halabi, part 3 pg 327.

changed in a way that could reflect badly on him, he tended to shift part of that chapter's verses into a different section or a different chapter and to add to it some phrases that served to increase its ambiguity, complexity and to make it more misleading.

Also Muhammad tended to add a lot of strange words originating either from different languages that were not understood by Arabs, or from his imagination. This addition used to correspond with the Quran Rhyme. Moreover, Muhammad added some scattered letters into the Quran to mislead Arabs. He gave complex and difficult instructions to his followers.

The stories of Jewish prophets, repetitions, that sometimes contradicted each other and exaggerations all served to complicate the Quran and confuse the reader. Muhammad also created statements that could be interpreted in multiple way; creating ambiguous abstracts that do not exist in the Arabic Language, for example:

'Whom he registered them as his wives!' – used to cover the correct number of Muhammad's wives,

'For those whose hearts have been (recently) reconciled (to the Truth)' - this is used to give money to his tribe Quraish.

'And to him who took on himself the lead among them' referred to Abdullah Bin Abi Salool, one of the strong tribe leaders who took the adultery scandal of Aisha and promoted and exaggerated the story. Muhammad punished weak people but was scared of the tribe leader Abdullah and he used the ambiguous term to prevent talking badly about Abdullah directly.

Secondly, in all world languages, in writing or talking about somebody, people are first referred to by name and then referred to by a pronoun (e.g. he or she). Muhammad's Quran begins a sentence with a pronoun and then later identifies the person being referred to in an ambiguous way. This style benefited Muhammad and later Muslim clergymen in identifying and changing those pronouns according to their needs and necessity. For example: Muhammad talks about women in his Quran in chapter 4, An-Nisa in verse 25 'if they fall into shame' – the pronouns are ambiguous, Muhammad is talking about a group of women without identifying them.

'Their punishment is half that for free women' and so, we first have to identify the free woman, to make it easier to know the first group of women he referred to. 'The free women' (translated into Arabic Mohassanat) refer to married women. Even this is a metaphoric identification for married women. So, from this verse, we understand that the adultery sin committed by an unmarried woman is measured as half of the same sin committed by a married woman. This meaning is incorrect, it is a literal linguistic explanation. As per the Bedouin traditions and values, the first group of women refers to slaves[12].

A great deal of literature exists that tries to explain Muhammad's Quran, each with its own theories and interpretations of the Quran's unfamiliar words, ambiguous pronouns and contradictory statements.

The ambiguity has meant that however well trained an Arab is in understanding the Quran, he or she cannot give a decisive answer on many issues after reading the complex, coded Quran. For example, if you argued that it is unfair that slave women were punished less, one could argue that that is not the case as Muhammad did not mention the word 'slave' at all in that sentence.

All that is left is for Islamic clergyman to interpret or explain the Quran as he likes and to authorise or prohibit actions based on this subjective interpretation.

---

[12] Ibn Kathir, pg 463.

# The chronological development of the Quran

At the beginning of Muhammad's religious mission in Mecca, he was a Hanif and entered several abstracts in his Quran. During this period, he wrote the Quran in a simple narrative style as shown in the peaceful Mecca verses. After the failure of this mission, Muhammad emigrated to Medina, where the Jews lived, and got to know the Jewish ways well. After this, he changed his Quran in a rhematic way, writing it in a style more like that of a clergyman or of the Torah. Muhammad was also introduced to the Hindus way of reading the holy book and although he did not understand what was said, he realized that this style was highly emotive and could influence the spirit, so he decided to use a similar way of reading while reciting the Quran.

In his Quran, Muhammad stated 'recite the Qur'an in slow, measured rhythmic tones'[13]. Muhammad called this way of singing as reciting in order to incite the emotions while listening to the Quran. That is why we find a considerable similarity in the way of reading the Quran by Muslims and the way of reading the Veda by Hindus.

---

[13] Quran, sura 73, Al-Muzzammil, the Enshrouded one, verse 4.

### Refusal to collect the whole Quran in One Volume

Muhammad refused to collect his Quran in one book or volume as he wanted it to remain as non-unified verbal instructions, distributed among many books. He ordered each scribe of the Quran to have his own copy of it, with all their differences and similarities. Nowadays, it is up to the Muslim individual to choose whatever suits him from those different Qurans, according to his understanding of life and what suits him.

The cunning of Muhammad meant that he could change his mind whenever he wished, as no one version of the Quran was definitive. What was true then is still true today – that no story or incident in the Quran can be reliably debated, as there is no unified source for obtaining the information.

If the Muslim was a strict Bedouin and a follower of the extreme thoughts like Wahabi, he would choose the Medina Verses which contain killing and violence and would say that the other verses are incorrect. Whereas, if the Muslim used to live in the ancient agricultural civilizations or harbours, he would chose the peaceful Mecca verses which promotes Islam by using dialogue and he would decline the existence of the violent verses, full of war and killing of captives, by saying that such verses have been introduced into the Quran to distort Islam image as a religion of love and tolerance.

These differences and the variety of the Quran versions among its writers led to a conflict among them during the lifetime of Muhammad. Here is what happened - Omar Ibn Khattab the second caliph said: 'during the life of Muhammad, I heard Hisham Bin Hakeem reading the Chapter of Forkkan and asked him *who taught you these verses*. 'Muhammad', Hisham replied[14]. *You are a liar*, I said to him because Muhammad taught me those verses. So I took him to Muhammad where I read the version of the chapter as I know it, Muhammad replied, *you are correct*, then Hisham read his version of the chapter, and Muhammad replied *you are correct.*'

Ibn Masood, one of Muhammad's Quran writers, said: 'I have heard a man reading a verse while Muhammad reading the same verse but in a different way, so I went to Muhammad to inform him and he told me - *both of you are correct and do not argue*.' [15]

Certainly, Muhammad prepared his excuses for these contradictions, which permitted the Muslim clergymen to follow, saying that the difference among the Bedouin dialects is the main reason for that, as the Quran has been taught in seven different Bedouin dialects. If you read the two previous sayings carefully, you will notice that Muhammad himself read the Quran before those writers, who in turn, listened to the same words, reading and accent from Muhammad. So these words were not written using their own Bedouin accent. The difference among the accents will lead to a slight change in the way of pronouncing the word. This kind of change would not have upset Omar and cause him to accuse Hisham of being a liar and then take him to Muhammad.

Following this, Ibn Masoud said that he felt that Muhammad hated this question and said 'I have seen it in his face that which implied do not ask this question again, write down what I say in your own Quran and do not bother with what others write or say in their Qurans, you are all correct'. This illustrates the way in which Muhammad refused to collect and unify the Quran in one book.

---

[14] Sahih Al Bukhari, Al Bukhari, chapter Repent of the rebellions, saying 6936.

[15] Sahih Al Bukhari, Al Bukhari, chapter The Prophets Sayings, saying 3476.

# Muhammad's insistence that he was a prophet

*I*t is apparent that Islam is a Hanif religion. Muhammad is the third generation of the Hanif from the dynasty of Abdulmotalib, Muhammad's Grandfather. Despite all these facts, Muhammad insisted that he is God's prophet.

Abdulmotalib represented the first generation of this dynasty in worshipping Allah without being connected with other statues, but this worship was accompanied by fear from the curse of the statues. Abdulmotalib had named his son Abdullah (which means the worshipper of Allah), the father of Muhammad, while he called his first son Abdul Al-Uzza (the worshipper of the Idol Al-Uzza the female pagan deity) Abu Lahab (the father of fire) this name was given by Muhammad, but his real name Abdul Al-Uzza indicates the fear among Bedouin of the goddess and statues, especially, Al-Uzza.

Muhammad represented the third generation of Hanifs in this dynasty. He used to worship Al-Uzza and to sacrifice sheep before it. He was not able to overcome his innate

Bedouin fear of this goddess until he became forty years old. Muhammad did praise Al-Uzza and other Allah daughters in his Quran for political reasons and in order to expand his influence, then when these verses became worthless, Muhammad got rid of them.

Muhammad tried to persuade the Bedouins that his religion was complimentary to and corrective of Christianity and Judaism. His trials were represented by praying towards Jerusalem and fasting Ashoura, which is also fasted by Jews to persuade Jews to follow him and embrace Islam.

Muhammad heard that there was a man called Baraa bin Maroor [16] who embraced Islam and prayed towards the Kaaba instead of Jerusalem. Muhammad liked this idea and waited until the death of this Muslim to perform the same ritual [17]. In changing the direction of praying towards the Kaaba, he was secretly obeying the will of his pagan uncle Abu Taleb, who had asked Muhammad on his death bed to glorify the Kaaba.

To ensure the continuity of trade in Mecca through the pilgrimage, this change also coincided with Jews' refusal of and sarcasm towards Muhammad.

As a result of the Jews' refusal, Muhammad changed fasting, deciding to fast the whole month of Ramadan as a Hanif, following the steps of his Hanif grandfather. Muhammad adopted his grandfather's regulations for fasting in Ramadan, staying in a Hiraa cave and feeding the poor during this month of fasting – he took his fasting timing from the Torah - staying in the mosque and feeding the poor during Ramadan. Regarding the fasting of Ashoura, he said it is optional but not obligatory, like Ramadan is. Thus Muhammad confirmed that Islam is a

---

[16] Al Seera Al Nabawuya(Al Halabiya) Khaffaji Al Halabi, part 2 pg 14.

[17] Quran chapter 2 the Cow, Al-Baqarah verse 144 we shall turn you to Qiblah 'direction' that will please you.

continuation of the Bedouin values and thought, without bringing anything new into it at all.

Muhammad had abandoned praying towards Jerusalem and fasting Ashoura and kept the holiness of the holy months, pilgrimage to Kabaa, sacrificing, fasting in Ramadan, running between Saffa and Marwa, stoning the devil and all the rituals that a Bedouin believes in. Muhammad exaggerated the holiness of the black stone as a part of worshipping stones and also by saying: 'who believes in the stone, this will protect him' as a recognition and confession by him in worshipping statues. In spite of all this evidence and his failure in persuading the Jews, Muhammad insisted that he was a prophet and the last prophet. For that, he massacred Jews in vast numbers, fought Christian neighbours in many organised wars and raids, leaving this difficult task for the Muslims who followed him to create new ways to prove that Islam is a continuity and correction of Judaism and Christianity.

## Crossing the line

Muhammad did not permit anyone to express any form of doubt in his prophecy or criticism of his actions. Anyone voicing doubt or criticism would be killed immediately. In the chapter Tawba of the Quran, the prohibited actions and their punishments are detailed. Muhammad enforced these punishments by sending his gangs to kill anyone opposing or criticizing him.

Muhammad was a Hanif, and yet he claimed he was a prophet of Allah. Lots of Hanifs were worried as he adopted and quoted most of their regulations, for they did not embrace Islam. This included his uncle Abu Taleb, who, although he lived and died as a pagan, provided protection to Muhammad.

When Muhammad emmigrated to Madina he started founding his armed Mafia, organizing raids, stealing and killing captives. The Hanifs condemned such barbaric behaviour, criticized Muhammad and refused his Islam, as they were the real founders of this religion for promoting peace and stopping civil wars among Bedouin tribes.

Umaya bin Al Salt, a prominent, senior Hanif [18], criticised Muhammad and his followers for their barbaric behaviour in a poem (when Ibn Hisham wrote Muhammad's biography, he did not include this poem, as Muhammad prohibited it). Muhammad did not tolerate any criticism, the punishment was burning books, prohibition or execution – just for mentioning the poem! Muhammad wanted to stop the communication among Islamic critics. This also acted as a form of mind control – by censoring people's words and actions, they would begin to censor their own thoughts and so over time come to believe more fully in Muhammad.

Abdullah bin Sareeh, one of Muhammad's scribes, was the only person who was saved from this punishment as Othman protected him.

Muhammad's ambiguity was accompanied by complexity, obscure coding, the availability of various different copies of the Quran, killing anyone who understood the real Islam and who he felt had crossed the line or opposed him and burning books criticizing Islam.

Today Muslim clergymen maintain the tradition of burning books and banning their distribution. They make this a higher priority over killing authors, in order to halt any cultural communication that might lead to founding a logical trend that refutes Islam on a scientific and historical basis. Unfortunately, many of the moderate Muslims and western authors think that such criminal acts spring from the personal beliefs of some extremists who are ignorant

---

[18] Systematic reading in Islam pg 30

about the message of Islam, which calls for love and tolerance and accepts dialogue.

Saying that Islam calls for love does not make the reality of Muhammad's message of hate and condemnation of critics to execution any less real. There are many books criticising all religions such as: Hinduism, Christianity, Sikh, Buddhism, Judaism, etc. – all except Islam. For example, neither was the book *The Da Vinci Code* burnt, nor was Tom Hanks killed, nor were there any violent demonstrations by Christians calling for executing the director or the author.

All religions can be criticised except Islam, within Islam, there is no place for tolerance. What is the reason behind all this fear of such critics? All other religions have been criticized and did not vanish because of it.

Muhammad himself and many real Muslims know the accurate details of the information contained in this book, and that Islam was built on fabrications and lies. Muhammad said 'the only fear I have upon my nation lies in its scholars, in case they become corrupt'. The words 'my nation' refers to the Arab world and not all the Muslims, as Muhammad was not scared of them. Muhammad was only scared of the Arab Scholars, but not of the Arab Muslim criminals, thieves and drunks. As those Arab Scholars understood the Bedouin mentality and had mastery of the Arabic language, Muhammad knew they could study his sayings and actions and reach the truth that Islam's regulations and values are based on violence and murder, as created by Muhammad to rule the Bedouins. This is why Muhammad refuses to let anyone criticize him, because the foundations of Islam are so weak, that one critical Arab could mean the end of Islam.

## Muhammad's relationship with Abu Sufyan

o justify raids on the Bedouin tribes, killing men and rafficking children and women as slaves, Muhammad symbolized himself as a protector of all poor people by transforming himself into a socialist fighter or a desert version of Robin Hood, who steals from the rich to distribute their wealth among the deprived to achieve a social equity.

In this battle, Muhammad created an opposing enemy symbolizing wealth and authority, he chose the Quraish tribal leader Abu Sufyan, who became the figurehead of this 'enemy'.

Abu Sufyan was Muhammad's political opponent in the fight between the evil 'Abu Sufyan' and the virtuous 'Muhammad'. Muhammad criticized Abu Sufyan and the Masters of Quraish in order to try and make his raids on their commercial campaign seem legitimate, but Muhammad, a tribal Bedouin, could not get rid of his loyalty to his tribe and his cousin Abu Sufyan. This loyalty was shown in the following sayings and actions:

- Muhammad refused to speak badly about Quraish. When his followers made exaggerations about assaulting Quraish, he said, 'these are my family.
- Muhammad insulted Hassan Bin Thabet, Muslim's poet, when he criticized Abu Sufyan saying 'how dare you insult him, he is my cousin!'
- When Abu Sufyan and the Quraish Masters accepted Muhammad's requests, they agreed to unite all Arabs living in the peninsula under the regime of Quraish (Islam).

Even after the unification of Muhammad and Quraish, Muhammad kept up the superficial façade of a struggle between himself and Abu Sufyan to justify the principle of equality and distribution of wealth. Abu Sufyan became one of the most dedicated protectors of Islam and Muhammad, he accepted the superficial criticism from Muhammad and the Muslims, provided that all ransoms were considered Quraish share. For this Muhammad had created the definition of 'For those whose hearts have been (recently) reconciled (with the Truth)'. All the stolen money, slaves and camels were given to Abu Sufyan and the Quraish.

The second condition that Abu Sufyan set was that the succession and the authority of Islam be granted to his heir, and this is what happened, Moawia Bin Abu Sufyan', the son of Abu Sufyan, became one of the caliphs. For this reason, Muhammad refused all offers from other Bedouin tribes to embrace Islam and to be part of his successors, in order to keep his promise to Abu Sufyan.

Musilamah, a prophet during the time of Muhammad, realized the political and military success that Muhammad had achieved after claiming prophecy and suggested to Muhammad to keep the issue of prophecy between them and then Musailamah should be his successor, but Muhammad also refused this proposal. [19]

One day, Moawia Bin Abu Sufyan heard someone say that a king would appear in the future from Kahttan and not from Quraish, which made him angry. He said that some people were promoting news not written in the Quran or in Muhammad's sayings, these people are ignorant and must stop these dreams that might mislead[20]. He continued 'I have heard Muhammad say that the authority will remain in the hand of Quraish only until the end of eternity or until the last two of them remain'[21]. Muhammad left this superficial criticism to Abu Sufyan, but there was a real danger that some Bedouin Muslims might believe that Abu Sufyan was a real enemy of Muhammad and could kill Abu Sufyan. For this reason Muhammad had to make firm and strict regulations to ensure the safety of his cousin Abu Sufyan. After the agreement between Muhammad and Abu Sufyan, according to which Muhammad's military forces should enter Mecca peacefully and without fighting, Muhammad demanded that his well known and distinctive mule should be ridden by both his Uncle Abbas and Abu Sufyan to ensure Muhammad's protection of Abu Sufyan[22],

Muhammad created a slogan in his campaign against Mecca that anyone who would enter the house of Abu Sufyan would be safe.

When Muhammad's army entered Mecca, the naïve Saad bin Abidah, from Medina, who was leader of a troop in Muhammad's army, believed that Muhammad wanted to occupy Mecca and that it was an actual war - not an agreed act between Muhammad and Abu Sufyan - that is why he said: 'today is an epic day, when a prohibited Kaaba will be

[19] Sahih Al Bukhari, Al Bukhari,chapter wars, saying 4378.
[20] Sahih Al Bukhari, Al Bukhari,chapter Al-Manaqib, saying 3500.
[21] Sahih Al Bukhari, Al Bukhari,chapter Al-Manaqib, saying 3501.
[22] Ibn Hisham part 4 pg 51.

destroyed and occupied'. But Muhammad was not impressed and gave his leadership of the troops to his cousin, Ali and said instead: 'today is the day of honour to Mecca'.

To cover up the superficial criticism of Abu Sufyan by Muhammad, the Muslim clergymen created funny stories about a secret agreement between Muhammad and Abu Sufyan in Medina before Muhammad entered Mecca, saying that Abu Sufyan came to Medina where he begged all of Muhammad, Abu Bakr, Omar, Ramla the daughter of Abu Sufyan (Muhammad's wife), Ali bin Abu Taleb and Fatima (Muhammad's daughter) to the degree that he asked the sympathy of Fatima by mentioning the name of her son Hussein, the grandson of Muhammad.

Clergymen here used the methods they had learnt from Muhammad to distort the facts, change history and attract people's attention elsewhere. Muhammad continued with the distorted Quran by exaggerating the punishment of hell and the status of infidels in his Quran, as we have seen. Such exaggeration can be found in his description of the visit by Abu Sufyan to Medina: in fact, weeks before Abu Sufyan's visit, a small delegation from Quraish had visited Muhammad and not Abu Sufyan, the master of Quraish. Muhammad did not believe it. In the end, Quraish accepted Muhammad as an opponent and wanted to speak to him. During this visit Muhammad lost control, became anxious and nervous, started to shout at his followers and dismissed a poor blind Muslim, Ibn Abi Maktoom. Later Muhammad took responsibility in the Quran for his bad behaviour by saying '(The Prophet) frowned and turned away, because there came to him a blind man (interrupting)'. This was his apology.

Can you believe that the daughter of Abu Sufyan refused to talk to her father? Muslim clergymen added to this a story in which Abu Sufyan, the tribal leader of Quraish, sat on the bed of his daughter Ramla and she said to him 'you dirt, don't you dare sit on the bed of the messenger of Allah'.

Muhammad and Quraish were not able to defeat the Thakeef tribe in Al-Taf, though they surrounded it for forty days, so Muhammad accepted Al-Taf's Master's conditions by praising their statues and encouraging Bedouin to visit their temple. Such encouragement was mentioned in Muhammad's Quran. This resulted in increasing the number of visitors to Al-Lat temple in Al-Taf town more than in the Kaaba in Mecca. Because of this, temples became the main opponents to Mecca and it became vital to get rid of them. Abu Sufyan and Mogeerah, a Muslim from Al-Taf destroyed statues (Al-Lat and Minna) and their temples taking Mogeerah to prove that this was a decision of Muhammad and Muslim nations and not Quraish only[23], later Muhammad and Abu Sufyan sent prominent Quraish master Khaled Bin Waleed to destroy the third temple where Al-Uzza used to be worshipped. In this way, the Kaaba became the only temple of worship on the Arab peninsula.

The naked pagan Bedouins had for over a year become used to praying in Mecca and to paying Muhammad their high tax (jizya). After the Tawba chapter, they were forbidden from making a pilgrimage to Mecca naked. Muhammad and Abu Sufyan destroyed temples and statues everywhere else except in Mecca, so Bedouins would worship only in the Kaaba temple in Mecca to worship the father of the statues, Allah, and to ensure the continuity of trade in Mecca with the pilgrimage.

After Muhammad's and Abu Sufyan's coalition to lead the Bedouins, Abu Sufyan was the leader in many battles such as the Al-Taf siege[24] where he lost one of his eyes, and

---

[23] Ibn Kathir, page1781.

[24] Al Seera Al Nabawuya(Al Halabiya) Khaffaji Al Halabi, part 2 pg 304.the footnote by Dahlan

the Yarmouk Battle against the Romans, which occurred after the death of Muhammad, where he lost his second eye and became blind for the love of Islam. Nowadays, the first thing that a child learns in the Islamic schools and curriculum is that Abu Sufyan is the enemy of Islam and Muhammad and that after the death of Muhammad, Abu Sufyan was delighted to know that Muslims were defeated in their wars to promote Islam, although Abu Sufyan had sacrificed both of his eyes for the love of Islam.

## Muslim Caliphs after Muhammad

Muslims who came into power after Muhammad, lived with him for more than twenty years and learned his style in deception, hiding information through code and creating complexity for the sake of it. They were experts in protecting their reign and changing the Quran and Hadith's interpretation to that which suited their own interests best.

The first Caliph, Abu Bakr, learned from Muhammad total loyalty to Quraish and Islam and to defend them unwaveringly. He appointed all the leaders from Quraish in his war against the revolting Bedouin tribes, denouncing Islam on the same day Muhammad died, regardless if those leaders were Muslim or infidel. He imitated Muhammad in the Honain Battle against the Hawazin tribe, Muhammad had enrolled Safwan bin Omaya, an infidel, in his army[25] and awarded him many prizes by the end of the battle. On the other hand, Muhammad refused to enrol non-Quarishi infidels in his army, as we have seen in a previous chapter.

---

[25] Ibn Kathir, page 888.

After the death of Muhammad, some of the Bedouin Muslim tribes remained Muslim, but refused to give either Abu Bakr or Quraish taxes. Abu Bakr said 'I will fight whoever discriminates between performing 'salat', (praying to Allah) and paying taxes to me'[26], i.e. he fought Muslims who prayed and did not pay the tax to him personally. Also, he said 'as the tax is an obligation, I swear on Allah that if they do not pay me tax, I will fight them even for the small camel that they used to pay to Muhammad'.

During Abu Bakr's reign, he was occupied with wars against revolting Bedouin tribes who opposed Islam. He remained the caliph for two years, adhered to his pledge to Muhammad and did not collate the Quran into one volume.

The second caliph, Omar, continued the same policy, but he explicitly banned temporary whoredom. Omar had frequently requested that Muhammad force women to wear hijab, but Muhammad had always refused. When Omar became Caliph, he changed and twisted the interpretation of words in the Quran and forced women to wear hijab. Omar also adhered to Muhammad's instructions not to collate the Quran into one volume.

The third caliph, Othman, was a rich merchant, but a weak leader, who was not able to force his authority upon the Bedouins by firmness or war. His reign was characterized by rebellions, instability, riots and revolutions. Othman appointed all his relatives as leaders, so scandals and embezzlement overwhelmed his reign. Othman tried his best to shed Muhammad's way, by placing the Tawba chapter in the middle of the Quran, also to improve his image, by collating the Quran into one volume and violating Muhammad's instructions in this regard. Although he took this daring step, Othman was assassinated by Ali in order that Ali could become caliph.

---

[26] Sahih Al Bukhari, Al Bukhari,chapter Al-alzakh, saying 1400.

In collating the Quran, Othman placed the Tawba chapter which is the last chapter said by Muhammad in the middle of the Quran, to hide it, instead of placing it in its correct place at the end of the Quran. Othman explained the reason behind this:

'I learned this from Allah's Messenger by transferring verses and chapters [27] – he meant he had learned from Muhammad how to lie and forge facts. He also said that Anfal chapter (the Jews' massacre) was the first chapter in Medina and the Tawba chapter was the last chapter in Medina and those two chapters are similar, so I placed them after each other.'

In fact the Tawba chapter is so scandalous, cruel and brutal that Muslims don't want to show that it was the last words and orders of Muhammad in his Quran.

The Tawba chapter deleted and cancelled in total 124 old Meccan verses as Allah changed his words as he wanted, which means that the Tawba chapter deleted and cancelled all the peaceful Meccan verses calling for dialogue, understanding and individual freedom in embracing Islam or not were all abrogated and cancelled.

I will take only 3 verses from those cancelled to show how Muhammad changed his words and orders in his Quran:

Chapter 39, the small group, Az-Zumar, verse 41:

He who comes to guidance does so for himself,
And he who goes astray does so for his own loss:
On you does not lie their guardianship.

Chapter 29 the spider Al Ankabut verse 46:

Don't argue with the people of the book unless in a fair way.

---

[27] Ibn Kathir, page 859.

Chapter 32 As-Sajdah verse 30:

Therefore turn away from them, And wait as they are waiting.

If a Muslim clergyman is involved in an interview or debate and claims that Muhammad's intentions were peaceful and that the violent verses cancelled the peaceful verses, this is a lie. There is overwhelming evidence that Islam and Muhammad are violent and aggressive

Because of the massive, well planned, complexity in understanding Islam and Muhammad, westerner's interviewers swallowed the Meccan verses in the Quran, not knowing the depth of lies behind these verses.

Othman kept all the cancelled, abrogated, peaceful Meccan verses and placed them at the end of the Quran, to deceive and persuade all naïve people, Muslims and non-Muslims alike, that those were the last instructions given by Allah and the last beautiful words that Muhammad uttered. In fact Othman should not have written the peaceful Meccan chapters at all, as we have seen in the story of Ibn Masood, Allah had sent Jibreel the ghost to erase the abrogated verse and not to write and collate them at the end of the Quran as Othman had done.

Nowadays, in Africa, Europe and North America, Muslim clergymen are able to convert many people who are deceived by Islam by reciting the last abrogated pages of the Quran. The clergymen also created a ridiculous explanation to justify Othman's intelligent fabrication by saying that the Quran was collated according to each verses' size, from the longest to the shortest. Most of the Meccan verses were written by simple poetry and were short verses, so the fabrication has some circumstantial evidence to support it, but how can we explain the two chapters – Maida (table) that consists of 120 verses and the Anfal chapter that consists of 75 verses, both placed before the Tawba chapter which consists of 129 verses.

Saying that Othman collated the Qu-an by the size of the verse also does nothing to explain why he would have collated them by size.

There was a huge number of verses and chapters for Othman to collate in one Quran. What actually happened is that Othman started studying their literary style and content, and every one which did not correspond with Othman's and the governing Quraish party's interests was omitted.

Aisha said during the days of Muhammad, that the Ahzab chapter consisted of 200 verses [28] but Othman reduced it to 73 verses! The Shiaa Party said that Othman omitted verses that did not correspond with his political interests[29]. For example, a whole chapter had been omitted, saying: 'those you believed and followed, Muhammad and his successor (the Shia here means Ali, Muhammad's cousin), who were sent to show you the right way of living, they are a prophet and his successor, both deputing each other,' As per Aisha, saying the number of the omitted suras and verses is so huge, those chapter and verses were written in some of the Qurans like in the Quran of Ibn Abbas and Abi bin Kaab[30] and can not be found in other Qurans, such as the chapter by Alkhal w Alhifid, that says: 'Allah we are asking for your help and forgiveness, we praise you and we do not stop believing in you. We will leave and we will not follow anyone who would blaspheme you. We pray to you and we seek your mercy and we fear your punishment.' The difference here is that in some of the Qurans there were very lengthy chapters, but these are not in other Qurans.

Furthermore, during the Othman era, when the Quran was collated, some of the parties who were suspicious about

---

[28] Al itikan Fi Uloum AlQuran: As Souyouti Part 2/ Pg25.

[29] Systematic Readings in Islam, pg. 86

[30] Al itikan Fi Uloum AlQuran:As Souyouti Part 1/Pg 65

the prophecy of Muhammad noticed the nature of some verses. The omitted chapter and verses were a prayer conducted by mankind to Allah, asking for forgiveness and redemption. So those verses were not Allah's words or instructions to clarify regulations. The speaker in the Quran compiled by Othman has to always be Allah, not somebody else, as shown in those omitted verses. Those prayers were performed by Muhammad later, he forgot that and changed them into the Quran. Muhammad knew all these technical difficulties and for this reason he refused to collate his Quran into one volume.

Even in Othman's volume of the Quran, there are many verses of prayer squeezed between other verses as in the Fatiha chapter, where there is a verse saying 'Show us the straight way'. This verse is repeated seventeen times a day by more than one billion Muslims asking for enlightenment from Allah, without noticing that those were human prayers and not Allah's word.

The rift among Muslims increased because of the omission of verses and chapters in the Quran. Abu Thar Al Gafari, a very prominent Muslim, objected to such manipulation of the Quran and decided to live in isolation, so as not to jeopardize the unity of Bedouin by Othman's Quran version[31].

The writer of Muhammad's biography in the book of Al Seera Al Nabawuya (Al Halabiya), Khaffaji Al Halabi covers up such facts by saying that there was a misunderstanding between Othman and Abu Thar Ghafari in interpreting some of the Quran verses, so the latter decided to live in isolation. When anyone reads this sentence, especially Muslims, they may believe that, but if they contemplated on it and thought of it as an interpretation of the Quran; Othman did not interpret the Quran, he only

---

[31] Al Seera Al Nabawuya(Al Halabiya) Khaffaji Al Halabi, part 2 pg 327 footnote by Dahlan

collated it. There have been many books interpreting the Quran, but none of them were written by Othman. The misunderstanding between Othman and Abi Thar Al Ghafari therefore had to be in collating the Quran, and not about its interpretation.

In conclusion, Muhammad began by keeping his options open and making it so he could rewrite the Quran as he wished. He passed on this method of forging and manipulating facts to his followers, who have passed it on to the Muslim clergymen of today, such that anyone with an honest desire to learn the truth hidden behind the Quran has to wade through 1400 years of ever changing facts based on lies and fabrications.

## The mingling of Arabian Bedouins and Islam with the rest of the nomadic tribes in the great nomadic arch

Arabian Bedouins were united under Islam, which aimed to expand and occupy areas outside the Arabian Peninsula by organized military raids carried out by Bedouins. The first encounter between Arab Bedouins and non-Arab nomadic tribes, living in the middle of the Asian mountains, took place in the early phase of Islam.

The nomadic tribes were easily convinced to embrace Islam. One reason for this is that it allowed them to continue carrying out raids and thefts; they saw that by joining Islam, they could continue with these activities under the pretext of spreading the word of Islam.

They recognised that Islamic principles were not so different from their own – they would continue to occupy new land, steal and destroy neighbouring civilizations, only now it would be through the guise of religious regulation.

The Asian nomads also enlisted in the Islamic army, whose leadership was always Arabic and whose orders were carried out by non-Arabian nomads who lived in the middle of Asia.

The second encounter between Islam and the rest of the nomadic tribes in the great nomadic arch took place when nomadic Moguls raided Baghdad, the capital of the Islamic empire, in a later phase of Islam. Moguls were introduced to Islam as a collection of nomadic thoughts, traditions and values based on occupying other territories and treating the rest of the peoples as slaves, which corresponded with their Mogul's nomadic principles and needs. Accordingly, Moguls embraced Islam to legitimise their action of occupation, theft and slavery using religious regulations.

The Muslim Mogul saw India as a precious treasure full of rivers, lands, farms, harbours and peaceful nations. This is why nomadic Muslim Moguls occupied India. When British troops occupied India, they freed Indians from those Muslim tribes and ended the Muslim mogul reign of India.

In spite of differences in language, race, origin and geography in the great nomadic Arch, the vast majority of its population embraced Islam easily because it corresponded with their nomadic principles and values. The only nomadic nation in this arch that did not embrace Islam were the nomads of Tibet. The Himalayan Mountains, being a huge geographical obstacle, made such mingling impossible, due to the harsh environment, topography and climate in those mountains.

Muhammad said 'if you prefer to be busy in trading and farming and leave Jihad (war), Allah will punish you with misery and humiliation. This punishment shall not be raised from you until you return and perform your Jihad'[32].

This prohibited nomads all over the world from working in trade or agriculture, mingling or learning from agricultural nations, becoming civilized and settling down instead of travelling and fighting, so nomads have to keep in

---

[32] Ibn Kathir, pg. 869.

their profession as warriors, shepherds, travellers, characterized by cruelty, terrorism and slavery.

Muhammad emphasised the aggressiveness and importance of using terrorism and cruelty in scaring and empowering civilized nations by saying in his Quran: 'Against them make ready your strength to the utmost of your power, including steeds of war, to strike terror into (the hearts of) the enemies of Allah and your enemies,'

After all different nomadic tribes in the great nomadic arch were united by Islam, the Islamic empire expanded from India in the east to Mauritania and Spain in the west. In order to study the influence of the mingling of Bedouin Arabs and Islam with other nomadic tribes and civilized agricultural nations; two countries shall be taken into consideration to see how Islam effected them.

## Turkey

Turkey lies in an advantageous location in the middle of a crossing point between continents and civilizations bordering the Mediterranean Sea. The first human population and civilization was in Turkey. Turkey has plenty of fertile agricultural land, harbours, cities, rivers, rain and a variety of geographical landscapes.

Turkey was a peaceful, stabilised, civilised, cooperative and open country in its dealings with the whole world. Istanbul was considered to be a universal capital and an intellectual, cultural, artistic and political opponent to Rome. Turkey had prosperity in trade, philosophy and art. When Muslims entered Turkey, they failed to get rid of this cultural and historical heritage and human communication and connection with the other civilizations, histories, thoughts and values. The Turkish nation and the Turks are proud of their cultural inheritance and appreciate previous civilizations as a means of cultural human communication without hatred or prejudice.

Nowadays, there is still difficulty in applying the principles of Islam and the Bedouins to the open and civilized nation of Turkey. Academically and intellectually, Turkey used to be a universal leader for many centuries, but aggressive Islamic principles set Turkey backwards, creating administrative corruption, wars, and a hatred of other nations.

This hatred has nothing to do with the personality of the Turks, as otherwise there would have been evidence of it before the entrance of Islam. Violence and aggressiveness are core Islamic teachings and it is these that brought the hatred.

Turkish intellectuals therefore turned to Atatürk to rescue Turkey from the ignorance of Islam, by deciding to get rid of Islam and of its Caliph; even if he was Turkish and governed the vast empire from Turkey.

Atatürk fought Islam frankly and openly at a time when Islam, the Quran and Muhammad were ambiguous secrets and when there was no literature against Islam based on historical and scientific evidence. He believed that Islam did not and would not bring anything to Turkey but ignorance and hatred, so he tried to regain Turkey's natural and historical position in Europe by being open to the whole world. Firstly, he abolished the Islamic caliph in Turkey and transformed Turkey into a modern republic. Secondly, he abolished the Arabic alphabet used for the Turkish language and adopted the Latin alphabet instead, thirdly he transformed the weekends into Saturdays and Sundays instead of Fridays, the Muslim holiday, and finally he founded a party that refused Islam, headed by Turkish intellectuals, authors, women and artists (this party still exists today).

All over the world, except in Turkey, military coups' leaders use religion to ensure the support of the majority. In

Turkey, military coups' leaders refuse Islam and carry out their actions with the support of intellectuals, both men and women. Turkish military coups aim firstly to stop establishing a new Islamic caliph era by Muslim clergymen; secondly to separate the Islamic religion and the Quran from the country and its constitution; thirdly to protect Turkish women's rights and not to force them to wear Hijab as in Iran, fourthly to be part of Europe and the European Union. These are the wishes of the population residing in the west of Turkey, where the percentage of illiteracy and unemployed women is very low. In the rural isolated villages, where poverty, illiteracy and ignorance are much greater (and more children and women wear Hijab), it is more common for residents to vote for the Islamic parties, to return back to the era of the caliph and to apply Muhammad's law literally.

## The Indian sub continent

Similar to Turkey, the Indian sub continent is a huge land encompassing fertile lands, rivers and seasonal rain, it is stable and civilised and has a variety of religions, races and languages. The Indian subcontinent has religious tolerance; no one is forced by violence to embrace a specific religion, even Hinduism, which is the largest religion in India, in which its followers have to be Hindu by birth. Islam, on the contrary, calls for expansion and each Muslim is obliged to introduce people into Islam, to transform the whole population of the world into Muslims, willingly or otherwise. All the Indian religions and cultures are located in peaceful and cooperative agricultural cities and towns that mingle with others and are filled with a variety of races and religions.

The Asian nomadic Muslim tribes, led by Arabs, carried out many raids against India. Muslims were faced with a variety of religions and races and violent opposition by Hindus who refused their ruling. The continuous raids caused both parties many losses. The nomadic Muslims were successful in occupying Hindu land, stealing their goods and burning their cities, but despite inflicting all this on the Hindus, the Hindus did not convert to Islam as a way of stopping this onslaught. The Hindus who kept their religion did however start to pay high tax (jizya) to their new masters. To this day, Hinduism still exists in India.

The second religion that Muslims faced on the Indian subcontinent was Buddhism, which is a religion embraced by millions of Indians and others, founded by Buddha more than 2500 years ago, based on a peaceful philosophy. Buddhists believe in the prohibition of killing any person, animal or even insects. Violence and force are prohibited completely.

Buddha was not aware of the dangers and violent powers surrounding the Indian subcontinent, the great nomadic arch, whose danger increased and multiplied after nomads embraced Islam and the different nomadic tribes were united under Islam.

Buddha was not aware either of the nomads' aim in life: travelling, shepherding, stealing and fighting over the limited sources to earn their living. Because of this way of life, they would not survive if they didn't enslave others. Buddhism as a principle lacks realism and practicality, which is why Buddhists suffered heavily during these raids as they refused to embrace Islam and also refused to fight Muslims. The Bedouin Muslims were astonished by the Buddhist's request to leave them contemplating in their temples, Muslims locked Buddhists inside their temples and burned them alive, or Muslims attacked Buddhists with their swords and killed them while they were meditating.

Muslims used to chase Buddhists on the Indian subcontinent and tried their best to avoid Hindus as much as possible. Some of the Buddhist cities and populations were safe from the Islamic destruction as they were located in areas surrounded by Hindus. A few Buddhists ran away to the remote mountains. For that reason, one might notice the random distribution of Muslims in the Indian continent. Pakistan and Bangladesh were Buddhist areas. Muslims occupied and stole Buddhist villages and cities, killing its men and capturing their women and children as slaves. Muslims forced all Buddhist children to embrace Islam to cut their connection with their origin, religion, culture and history and to increase the number of Muslims in these areas, as per Muhammad's orders due to the Islamic need for fighters to occupy the other nations and civilizations.

The new generation of Muslims (formerly the children of Buddhists) did not have any respect for their previous culture and religion and were convinced that they were naked cannibals, living in the forests without any civilization or history and that Islam had transformed them from this state to civilized individuals. The nomadic Muslims massacred Buddhists far more than any other people they attacked, but the latter until now refused to talk about these massacres because their religion forbids them from hurting others, even though they almost wiped out the Buddhists.

Tibet was the only nomadic nation that did not embrace Islam because of its harsh geography; the Tibetans were the most violent nomads in the whole arch, and they occupied all of Asia and large parts of the Chinese and Indian Civilizations' lands. A King of the Tibetans wanted to unite his vast empire under one religion. He chose Buddhism and forced the Tibetan nomads to embrace it. Later, the Tibetans became an easy target for other nomads in the arch, so the Moguls took control over them for many centuries.

In time, the Bedouin Arabs' leadership started to weaken and to lose control over their territories. A fight for power among Muslim nomads resulted in massacres, cruelty and the like. If you studied the life of any Muslim prince, king or sultan in any historical era or area within the Islamic empire, you will see how he seized authority from the previous king or sultan, using either conspiracy or murder, regardless of if he was his brother or father.

The Indian sub continent faced another wave of violence from the nomadic Moguls at a later stage. Moguls converted to Islam and adopted its method of expansion by stealing land and occupying it. Moguls occupied India and, as the Moguls were Muslims, the Muslim Indians (formerly Buddhists) were the privileged class, full of leaders, traders and wealthy people. When the British troops occupied India and ended the Mogul empire, the Muslims lost their privilege and wealthy life.

There was a disconnection from the previous culture in the first phase because of the occupation of India by Muslims from the west, and also in the second phase because of the occupation of Muslim Moguls from the north east in India, along with Muslim prosperity. The Muslims from the Indian subcontinent became more proud and committed to Islam than any other nation. They adored Arabs who founded this religion and taught them the Arabic language and civilization.

In 2001 Al-Qaida destroyed statues of Buddha in Afghanistan. This mission was executed by Afghani and Pakistani Muslims for whom their old civilization does not mean anything. This destruction was planned by Egyptian people like Thawahiri. Why did he not destroy the ancient Egyptian statues located in each corner of Egypt? Any Egyptian person, even Thawahiri himself, is proud of the old Egyptian civilizations and statues and its humane and intellectual values, even if they were worshiped at a certain time. These statues are respected by most of the Muslims in Egypt, Turkey, and Persia, while Muslims from Indian sub continent despise and refuse to know anything about Buddhist statues and their old civilizations.

For Muslims from the Indian subcontinent, Islam is their identity, origin, history and inheritance and they consider anyone referring to Islam negatively as a personal insult. This is associated with the super privileged position of the Arabic person and Arabic language. For this reason, most of the demonstrations that support Islam in western cities are carried out by Muslims from the Indian subcontinent; with an Arabic leadership as per Muhammad's instruction. In those demonstrations a participation of Turkish or Iranian Muslims is rarely noticed.

In Turkey there is a struggle between big Turkish cities that refuse Islam and remote isolated villages that adhere to Islam. In Pakistan there is a struggle between two types of Islam: firstly, Wahabi conservative Islam located in the North West of the country, close to Afghanistan, where the great nomadic arch passed. This area is inhibited by nomadic tribes, characterized by continuous civil wars, lack of safety, terrorists' centres and the spread of Wahabi Islamic schools. Secondly the Sufi tolerant Islam located in southern areas of the country where the big harbours and agricultural civilization, Sufi aims at tolerant, moderate Islams.

Pakistanis believe that Islam is the sole right path for a good future for Pakistan, but the dilemma is, which type of Islam will lead the country?

Unlike some other nations, the Turkish nation faces a great difficulty in accepting Islam. The nation of Saudi Arabia and the Gulf countries accepted Islam easily because it is the continuity of their Bedouin values. If an opposition arises within the Gulf nations, usually its aims is to apply a more conservative approach.

## What Biographers of Muhammad and Islamic authors learned from Muhammad and Muslim Caliphs.

The Islamic empire became huge and many nations were forced to embrace Islam, either through violent action, in order to stop paying the high tax (jizya) or by being despised and excluded in their society. Thousands of books were written about Muhammad and Islam by Arabs and others. Those authors had learned a lot from Muhammad and the Muslim caliphs about hiding Islamic flaws. They falsely praise Muslim governors and Muhammad by exaggerating their greatness, forging and fabricating facts to hide the faults of Muhammad and his flawed and brutal life. The methods used to achieve this can be categorized into three main ones:

1. Removing chronological clues, resulting in confusion in understanding the sequence of and reasons for specific incidents. Muhammad applied this method when he inserted Meccan verses among Medina ones and Othman applied the same method when he collated the Quran and placed the peaceful abrogated Meccan verses at the end of the Quran.
2. Using repetition and insertion of unrelated stories and poems to the subject. Muhammad applied this method when he repeated the description of heaven, hell, punishment and the prophets' stories.
3. Using legends, superstitions and witchcraft in their writing. This method was applied by Muhammad when he mentioned Genies, magicians and their stories in his Quran, for example he said in his Quran that he divided the moon into two halves and placed each half on a mountain.

This method was witnessed surely by Abu Bakr and Omar. The Author of the *Halabi biography* also used this third method. He included the following facts in the biography:

- Abdul Motaleb, Muhammad's Grandfather, asked for prohibition of adultery, drinking alcohol and amputation of thieves' hands.
- Abu Taleb, Muhammad's uncle, prohibited himself from drinking alcohol but he and his oldest son Taleb neither believed in Islam nor embraced it.
- After the death of Abu Taleb and Muhammad's marriage with the old rich widow and his improved financial status, Muhammad's young cousins, Ali and Jaffar, were raised by Muhammad and embraced Islam.

However, having included these three facts, he then used superstition in the chapter to prevent the reader from taking the above facts seriously, by saying that Taleb did not embrace Islam but was taken by a Genie![33] This hid the fact that he was killed and died as a pagan fighting Muhammad in the Bader battle.

Let's study some of those books:

The Quran's interpretation books, Tafsser Quran

Even Arabic intellectuals cannot understand the Quran without interpretation and most of the time, not even with interpretation. One of the books that interprets the Quran is: *Interpretation of the Quran* by Ibn Katheer, which contains 2061 pages of small print, the equivalent to 6,000 pages of normal size print. It is full of repetition, stalling and exaggeration. It gives more than four to five different, contradicting opinions in defining the simplest word in the Quran. The book is also full of stories that are unrelated to the Quran, contradictions, discontinuity and irrelevancies.

---

[33] Al Seera Al Nabawuya ,Part 2 Pg 288  foot note by Dahlan

To read Muhammad's Hadith, refer to Saheeh Bokhari, which contains 1,456 pages of small print, the equivalent of 4,500 pages of normal size print. This book is full of repetition, is written in an old and difficult version of Arabic, is highly tedious and takes a long time to read and understand.

To read Muhammad's biography, refer to Sirat Ibn Hisham, which covers 1,300 pages of small print, the equivalent of 3900 pages of normal size print. The book is full of unrelated poetry, names, stories and people. The number of names mentioned in this book is higher than that in the Iliad by Homer. It is also written in an old and difficult Arabic language.

Accordingly, the Arabic reader who wants to understand Islam has to read Muhammad's biography, Hadith and the Interpretation of his Quran, i.e. 14,000 pages of books, full of legends and superstitions used to carefully prevent Muslims from understanding Islam, so the Muslim reader practices his religion without understanding.

As evidence of this, Muhammad said that 'looking at the Quran is worship' so there is no need to understand or read it. To understand it, you also need to read Arabic – using Arabic dictionaries explaining the old Arabic language and words for the native Arabs themselves. So how will the non-Arabic Muslims understand Islam and Muhammad? When shall both Arabic and non-Arabic Muslims find time to read such volumes of books? Unfortunately, the authors of those books learned from Muhammad ways of filling their books with stories, superstitions, ambiguity and deleting the chronological sequence of incidents. These are some of the reasons for Islam's continuity as Muslim clergymen monopolized the trade of Quran interpretation, explaining Islam and the life of Muhammad.

## Reciting the Quran

uhammad said in his Quran: 'and we have rehearsed it to thee in slow, well-arranged stages, gradually'. This way of reciting was adopted from Hinduism to add to the experience of holiness when listening to the Quran. After Muhammad, the Muslim clergymen created long lists of complicated rules for reciting that require undergoing training for months to read it in a recital. Readers of the Quran are therefore now parrots with nice voices, singing the Quran without understanding its meaning. The parrots concentrate only in following complicated laws of reciting. Listening to recitals of the Quran is similar to listening to a song without concentrating on what it means, so when Muhammad said in his Quran: 'O Prophet! If a believer woman offered her body to the Prophet, if the Prophet wishes to have sexual intercourse with her, it is up to him, if he has, she should share no bed with other men[34]. The listener of this verse will start to cry and weep without understanding the meaning of

---

[34] Quran, sura 33, Al-Ahzab, the Clans, verse 49.

this verse; Muhammad meant that women have to offer their bodies to him. If Muhammad wanted to sleep with them without engagement, dowry or marriage, these women are only for Muhammad and he has the right to use them.

Non-Arabic Muslims are learning the Quran by heart but can not say 'Good morning' or 'How are you?' in Arabic! They do not speak Arabic, but have to pray and read the Quran in Arabic. This is one of Muhammad's strict orders.

Most of the westerners ask Muslims questions about their religion, thinking that Muslims understand it. Unfortunately Muslims, Arab and non-Arab, do not understand even the simplest things about Muhammad's biography, Hadith and the Quran. Information mentioned in my book about Muhammad and Islam is unknown and hidden to Muslims by Muslim clergymen, as was Muhammad's intention. By clergymen I mean clergymen in the Azhar Mosque in Cairo, who know the real stories about Muhammad and his Quran and fabricate different facts and hide Muhammad's mistakes. I don't mean Imams of mosques in the west who are busy collecting money from wedding contracts, Quran recitals and conducting prayers in religious rituals. Muslims are victims of Islam, a huge circle of lies and fabrication for more than 1,400 years, supported by thousands of books.

**Permitting Muslims to criticize Islam**

Muhammad was a shepherd with limited education, consequently his Quran was full of linguistic and grammatical errors. Muslim clergymen were permitted to criticize these mistakes, thus hundreds of books were written about these mistakes, but clergymen were not permitted to criticize the messages in the Quran, therefore all these books do is serve to distract attention from the truth of Islam and Muhammad's life. Indeed, many of them conclude that all these linguistic mistakes do is prove that the Quran is a miracle, because Muhammad could not have written it without Allah's help!

## Translation of the Quran into European languages

To Jews and Christians, Muhammad failed to prove that he was a prophet Islam is a continuity of Judaism and Christianity, therefore, Muhammad's successors and the rest of the Muslims have to learn from Muhammad's experience and try to succeed in the mission to convince them otherwise.

After the discovery of oil in Wahabi Arabian Gulf countries and the increase of its price, these countries have become wealthy and powerful. These countries and their governments depended heavily on Muslims from the Indian subcontinent who extensively studied the Torah and the Bible to issue new interpretations of the Quran – alongside the old ones – and to write books supporting Islam in European languages. Those translators are Muslims, eager to receive the generous payments from Arabian Gulf countries and ready to add and distort Allah's sayings. Those clergymen faced a big problem in translating the prayers of Muhammad in the Quran, pretending that they were Allah's words, although the speaker in it is human and is addressing Allah. To solve this problem, translators added the verb 'say' in translating the prayers, to refer to Allah ordering Muslims to say such prayers, even if this verb does not exist in the actual verse in the Quran.

Translations of the Quran using the same language, words, verbs, articles and style of the Bible and the Torah were very successful in Europe and North America and some of the citizens of these countries converted to Islam, as they believed that this translation represented actual words from Allah.

Due to this well fabricated translation, at the beginning of the last century, western authors noticed similarities between Islam, Christianity and Judaism and wrote literature that served Muhammad and Islam by introducing a unified definition of the three religions (Monotheism). Finally, Muslims were able to convince the whole world that Muhammad is a prophet and Islam is a great religion that complements Christianity and Judaism.

The translations do not indeed reflect the actual word and meaning of the Quran; for example, the word intercourse was translated as fornication; which was the same word used in the Ten Commandments. This word does not reflect the language used by Muhammad and his followers. He used a common vulgar word which translated as (did you fuck her) as mentioned in Saheeh Bokhari's book[35], so the term fuck has been translated into fornication. Another example, Quran chapter 33 Al-Ahzab verse 49 Muhammad said in his Quran:

'O Prophet! If a believer woman offered her body to the Prophet, if the Prophet wishes to have sexual intercourse with her, it is up to him, if he has, she should share no bed with other men.'

Look how Muslims translate this verse 'O Prophet! We have made lawful to any believing woman who dedicates her soul to the Prophet if the Prophet wishes to wed her; this only for thee, and not for the Believers (at large)', you can see very clearly the scale of falsification and fabrication.

---

[35] Sahih Al Bukhari, Al Bukhari, chapter fighting infidel, saying 6824.

## Influence of conqured cultures on Islam

he Islamic empire had increased after the enrolment of the vast majority of nomadic tribes in the great nomadic arch, stretching from India in the east to Spain in the west. Arab philosophers in Spain were influenced by Greek literature and wrote many books inspired by it, which they distributed to the largest Islamic cities such as Cairo and Damascus, while Arabs in the eastern parts of the empire were introduced to Indian literature.

Those two different schools of thought and literature poured into the capital of the Islamic empire, Baghdad. This era was called the 'Translation Era' in Arabic History, where many schools and trends appeared, calling for the use of studying, contemplating and reading literature, including sharing the thoughts and experiences of other nations to help write one's own literature. These intellectual trends were called Sufi; derived from the Greek word 'philosophy'.

The Sufi in the Greek part calls for reading and benefiting from experiences of other nations and developing those experiences and thoughts to help create new thoughts and to write and publish books. Accordingly, a new career was introduced in Baghdad: Waraq, which means a person who rewrites books to sell them for the benefit of the author.

Sufism, in the Indian regions, also calls for critical thinking, reading and writing, plus connecting all these activities with daily spiritual rituals and practices, to become part of a daily routine. Some of these practices and rituals that Muslims learned from Indians include fighting the physical and material instincts by mortification, abstaining, fasting, isolation, contemplation and reflection for many days throughout the year.

In Hinduism and Buddhism, the person usually contemplates by repeating one holy magical sentence a hundred and one times, and stops in that number of repetitions due to its holiness. Such repetition leads to relaxation and happiness. Muslims noticed that these words are not magical and any sentence repeated for more than one hundred times can lead to relaxation. For this reason Muslims altered these Indian words into 'Allah is alive' and 'there is no God but Allah'.

Indians use beads to ensure that when they repeat the magical sentences for one hundred and one times only, they stop due to the holiness of this number, so Muslims adopted the same ideas of beads, repetition and a holy number, along with serials of fabrications for its holiness, saying that the number one hundred and one is an odd number and it represents Allah the one and only. Also the holy number sometimes changed to ninety nine, as it represents the holy names and attributes of Allah according to Muhammad.

The Muslims also adopted the applications and practices of African religions and rituals. As millions of Africans were captured as slaves during the expansion of the Islamic empire, Arabs noticed African dances and drum beats while practicing their rituals. At the end of these rituals, Africans also feel relaxed and happy. Consequently, Muslims mixed the repetition of holy sentences with the African rituals and created the dervish movement, dancing, beating drums and repeating sentences such as 'Allah is alive' and 'there is no God but Allah'. Some of these dervish bands introduced the usage of knives and inserting them into the body, imitating some of the Indian sects.

Islamic Sufism became varied in its rituals and practice. When the Greek and Indian versions of Sufism were introduced to Baghdad, they represented a danger for Islam as they wanted to change Islam by calling for thinking instead of copying, tolerance and love instead of violence and slavery.

Sufism then transformed into a political philosophy, fighting the power of the Quraishi Caliph in Baghdad. Followers of Sufism were many such as AlRomi, Omar AlKhayyam and AlHallaj.

AlHallaj (born c. 858 A.D.) was considered a Sufi pioneer as his grandfather was Zoroastrian and he was Persian, he lived for nine years in India, learning principles of Hinduism and Buddhism and he was one of the most famous imams and poets in Baghdad. In his poetry, he called for love, tolerance and respect for others. He also praised Muhammad and Islam, but on the other hand he wanted to break the stiffness of Islam by using methods of thinking and debating.

He declared before his students that the Quran is not immortal and does not fulfill the needs of mankind in every era, but only in the era of Muhammad.

This declaration was considered a threat to the power of the Quraishi Caliph in Baghdad, as it implied that Muhammad is not a prophet, his Quran is not from Allah but his own creation, and the governing right of Quraish as granted by Allah is invalid. The caliph asked Hallaj to condemn these sayings and to confirm that the Quran is immortal or he would be crucified on the gates of Baghdad, but AlHallaj refused and was punished by crucifiction. Muslim clergymen fabricated a story about how the Muslim Caliph had legislated the killing by crucifiction of AlHallaj by saying: 'AlHallaj said that he is truthful, ignoring the fact that 'Truthful' is one of Allah's names and attributes, so AlHallaj was an infidel by saying he is Allah'.

After this, the Islamic authorities and Muslim clergymen declared a fierce war against Sufism to stop this intellectual, political and philosophical danger. They burned their books and the followers of Sufism were accused of heresy, disbelief and of being Shu'ubiyya (republicans). (Shu'ubiyya is any thought or trend aiming to coup against the authority of Muslim Arab Caliph granted by Allah from non-Arab nations. The non-Arab nations did not have the right of self-ruling).

Ultimately, Sufism failed to topple Islam, mainly due to the Mogul attack on Baghdad and the burning of their literature. Islamic Sufism, as taken from the Greek, was an intellectual movement full of philosophy and analytical thought, while the Indian part was calling for contemplation and daily practices. Muslim clergymen fought the intellectual version of Sufism – represented by analytical thought, writing and reading – and encouraged the contemplative version, emptying it from any thinking activities and filling it with dancing, fasting, singing and repetition, so Sufis nowadays are parrots able to sing, dance and learn by heart poems of Omar Alkhayyam, AlRomi and AlHallaj without understanding their real meaning, being full of love, tolerance and respect for others. They think that Muhammad was calling for these principles and words, not Buddha.

Muslim clergymen were successful in degrading Sufism and connecting its meaning to the word 'wool' in Arabic, called 'Suf'. While Sufis were successful in creating the word 'Elmani', meaning the person who believes in the power of science, not superstition, instead of using the word infidel. 'Elm' in Arabic means science and until now the non-believer of Muhammad is called 'Elmani'. Clergymen are trying to disconnect the concepts of science and heresy from each other.

# Interpretation of the Tawba Chapter

*I* would like to interpret the chapter Tawba (or At-Taubah, the Repentance, chapter 9), the last words and orders from Muhammad before he died, in the light of the information    presented in this book and with an understanding of the political and economic conditions at the time this chapter was written. This chapter includes a political speech expressing the anger of Muhammad against Muslims and only Muslims, which is why Othman hid it in the middle of the Quran.

## The political conditions

Muhammad used to receive a high tax (jizya) from the pagan Bedouin tribes for more than a year after his success in occupying Mecca. The Muslim clergymen do not mention the pagan infidels who made naked pilgrimages and who used to pray alongside the Muslim pilgrims in Mecca. This indicates that the main focus of Muhammad was on collecting more money, rather than on Allah, the Kaaba, the Quran, Halal, haram or to fight heresy. Those are words that Muhammad used to reach his political goals.

**Political opposition against Muhammad**

A political opposition against Muhammad emerged mainly due to the financial and administrative corruption, suspension of Muhammad's prophecy and the extremity of Quraish privileges by using all the stolen money and taxes for themselves. Abbas bin Mardas, a non Quraishi poet, said "I was fighting hard in a war with Muhammad and I was not given anything, not even a small camel"[36].

The emergence of Muhammad's political ambition was also a supporting factor in his decision to claim prophecy, particularly after his failure to defeat Al-Taf and acceptance of their conditions - continuing in pagan worship, praising their statues and receiving their high taxes (jizya).

Opponents of Muhammad ridiculed this prophecy and his Quran and encouraged Muslims not to enrol in his armies. The centre of this Opposition was a Mosque in Medina, later called 'Dirar Mosque' by Muhammad which means bad Mosque.

The opposition included a plan to kill Muhammad, to get rid of him, his Islam and Quraish.

**Economic conditions**

Through Islam, Muhammad united the Bedouin tribes on the Arabian Peninsula and stopping their civil wars.

---

[36] Ibn Hisham part 4 pg 146.

Consequently, sources of revenues from these tribes ceased as they stopped paying the jizya high tax.

Pagan Bedouin tribes continued to pay high taxes to Muhammad to ensure their security and safety, so Muslim Bedouin tribes could not attack each other and neither could pagans, Muhammad fully controlled the Arabian Peninsula.

Ibn Hisham said in describing the economic conditions of the time: it was a time when food and money were rare[37].

The economic state deteriorated to the edge of famine. Ibn Katheer said 'at that time two men were sharing one piece of date between them, sucking its water frequently'[38]. Muhammad found that the solution of this dilemma was occupying nearby civilised nations and expanding to feed the hungry Bedouin tribes. This was Muhammad's plot: uniting the Bedouin, then starving them to near death so that this would ignite dreams of war and of stealing from nearby nations, the Romans and Persians, to quell this hunger.

**The Persian Empire**

Persians were living near the Bedouins and the desert and knew the Bedouin mentality, as their capital was on the edge of the desert. The two parties therefore signed agreements and treaties to ensure the safety of Persia from Bedouin raids. Persia also controlled Yemen and Bahrain militarily and politically at that time; Muhammad had to demolish these bases before attacking Persia, which was exactly what happened later after the death of Muhammad.

---

[37] Ibn Hisham part 4 pg 169.
[38] Kathir, pg. 914.

## The Roman Empire

The Roman Empire consisted of many races and origins; its capital, Rome is located far away from the Bedouin desert. Romans were not aware of Bedouins and the danger of their unity and desperation due to starvation. The Roman Empire did not have any interest in the Arabian Peninsula, except for a few trading routes and limited commercial relationships between Mecca and Damascus. Muhammad decided to fight the Romans with his starved troops in a military campaign called Tabook.

The Bedouins thought that Muhammad aimed only at being king among Arabs and his speech about occupying Rome and the white palace in Babylon was a far flung plan unlikely to be carried out, so they did not take Muhammad's preparation to fight the Romans seriously, as they knew that he would be defeated. Apparently, they did not understand the real meaning of Muhammad's saying: 'I have been sent to kill humans till they say there is no god except Allah and Muhammad, Allah's messenger'. He did not specify a single people, he did not say 'I have been sent to kill Bedouins' or 'Arabs' so he was literally fighting everybody who didn't believe that he was Allah's messenger. This was a big misunderstanding by the Bedouin tribes.

Political opposition to Muhammad emerged with those who stated that they believed in Islam in order to avoid being killed by Muhammad and Quraish[39], but whose true belief was superficial, or non-existent. This opposition movement successfully convinced people not to participate in the army or support his war financially and promoted among Bedouins the message that if Muslims went to fight Romans they would be executed and hung on the gates of Damascus.

---

[39] Ibn Hisham part 4 pg 179.

This opposition also said that what motivated Muhammad's prophecy and goals was to expand politically and personally in his ambition to be a master. As a result of this opposition campaign, many Muslim Bedouin tribes refused to enlist in Muhammad's army and many Bedouin tribes refused to pay extra taxes to finance Muhammad's campaign against the Romans. Muhammad therefore lost financial support, weapons, horses and proper troops. By this time he was unable to enrol his hungry homeless wretches (Ahl Assafah) who were fierce fighters and who had been placed in the forefront of the army during his earlier wars against the Bedouin tribes. These wretches' own living consisted of participating in wars, looting and stealing. This is the main reason behind the failure of this campaign.

On the other hand, the Bedouins were afraid of Muhammad's sword and the anger of the Quraish, so they decided to go with Muhammad's campaign against the Romans and withdraw before the start of the battle. As a consequence, the psychological status of the army was affected, with troops driven by fear, but inside feeling Muhammad and the Quran were ridiculous, the lack of supplies and the increasing temperature. Omar described the situation saying that they were thirsty to the degree of death.

After twenty days of marching Muhammad became aware of the agreement among the Bedouin tribes to withdraw from battle and to get rid of him[40] as in the battle of Ohod, when Abdul Allah Bin Abi Salool withdrew with his troops before the battle resulting in the defeat of Muhammad. Muhammad came close to being killed in this battle, when a stone hit his head.

Omar realized the repetition of the same scenario was highly likely, so he advised Muhammad to withdraw and he

---

[40] Ibn Kathir, pg. 873.

did - but Muhammad said he withdrew on orders from Allah and not Omar!

Muhammad knew the existence of a huge resistance among his troops and the hatred of the Bedouins for him, so he took some precautions to avoid assassination.

In this military campaign Muhammad banned Muslims from drinking from oases and springs in the desert[41] and he had to be the first one to reach and drink from these water sources[42], just in case someone might poison the water. On two occasions, however, the Muslims drank water before Muhammad, who got furious and started to swear at the Muslims and curse them.

Due to the harsh topography of the routes that the army used, Muhammad banned his army from walking with him on narrow paths. In spite of all these strict regulations, the opposition did not hesitate to execute an assassination plan.

## The assassination attempt in the night of Aqaba[43]

On the way back to Mecca the army reached a narrow path called Aqaba at night. Muhammad announced that he would go through the path, while the whole army should pass through the wide valley. Muhammad was accompanied by two bodyguards, Ammar Bin Yaser and Hothaifa bin yamman. When the opposition heard this announcement, they sent 12 knights who rushed through the Aqaba path to surprise Muhammad and push him into the valley.

While Muhammad was passing the path, he heard the sounds of their horses and hid immediately, ordering his

---

[41] Kathir, pg. 895.

[42] Seera Al Nabawuya(Al Halabiya) Khaffaji Al Halabi, part 2pg 328,332, footnote by Dahaln.

[43] Al Seera Al Nabawuya(Al Halabiya) Khaffaji Al Halabi, part 2pg 333 and also Ibn Kathir, pg. 859.

bodyguards to attack. The plan failed and the attackers ran away and mixed with the army. Muhammad then asked his body guards if they knew any one of the knights. They said they did not, as they were disguised and in the dark, but they identified their horses. Hothaifa asked Muhammad about the reason of the attack. Muhammad replied the attackers wanted to attack me in the Aqaba and throw me into the valley and kill me, then Muhammad asked his bodyguards not to spread the news among the troops.

The next morning, Osaid Bin Hothair visited Muhammad and asked him the reason behind not passing through the valley, instead of taking the difficult narrow path. Muhammad informed him about the failed assassination attempt.

Osaid asked for their names to behead them, but Muhammad said that he did not want to fight his own people. In reality, Muhammad did not wait and he interrogated the knights who carried out the plan[44].

Muhammad did not punish them on the way back, saying that Allah would punish them instead by throwing Dabeelah at them – a word that did not exist in the Arabic language, but was created by Muhammad to scare Bedouins – later he explained that Dabeelah means a meteor of fire falling into their hearts and killing them. Actually Muhammad did not punish them immediately to avoid more riots among his troops, but when he returned to Medina he was informed that these knights were the political opposition group which used to gather in the Dirar Mosque.

---

[44] Muhammad was very angry and furious he said that in his Quran in verse 74, in the same chapter, Tawba. They turned unbelievers after having come to faith, and designed what they could not accomplish.

On the way back to Medina he renewed his previous treaties with the Christians[45] about paying high tax (jizia) to him.

When he arrived at Medina he ordered the burning and destruction of the Dirar Mosque [46] and houses of the opposing knights[47]. Secondly he discharged the head of one tribe from his position[48] and appointed one of his followers instead. Thirdly he sent an envoy to persuade Thakeef tribe in Al-Taf to destroy the temple of Al-Lat and to end its rituals and pilgrimage; to ensure that the Kaaba was the only destination for pilgrims.

The People of Al-Taf refused Muhammad's proposal and killed his envoy[49]. Their motivation for this was largely due to the recent increase of the visitors to the Al-Lat Temple and the increase of their incomes – after Muhammad had praised their statues in his Quran and encouraged the Bedouins to visit the Al-Lat temple.

Muhammad was angry with the Muslims who withdrew from his war, refused to participate in the first place, or who refused to fund his campaign. Muhammad threatened the political opposition with the punishment of death, then mutilating their hearts. Muhammad did not have any disagreement with the Christian and pagan tribes that paid their high taxes. He was only angry with the Takeef tribe in Al-Taf who killed his envoy, so he sent a clear message stipulating destruction of the Al-Lat temple and ending the ritual visits within a specific period. Muhammad then decided to change his previous decision in the Quran which says 'to you be your Way, and to me, mine'.

[45] Al Seera Al Nabawuya(Al Halabiya) part 2 g 333 footnote by Dahlan and Ibn Hisham part 4 pg 179.
[46] Ibn Hisham part 4 pg 184.
[47] Ibn Hisham part 4 pg 170.
[48] Ibn Kathir, pg. 885.
[49] Ibn Hisham part 4 pg 191.

Muhammad abrogated all the peaceful Meccan chapters and stated the new decision that all Bedouins have to become Muslims if they wish or not, within a specific period, and any Bedouin opposing this decision shall be killed.

## Orders of Muhammad stated in Tawba chapter.

As paying 'zakah' (low tax) by Muslims solely did not satisfy the needs of Muhammad. Muhammad deleted all the previous agreements with the Muslim Bedouin tribes that used to pay 'zakah', so that those tribes had to pay more money. Muhammad introduced a new tax he named 'sadakat' (charity) which was to gain Muhammad's forgiveness. This new tax money was obligatory, as per Allah's instructions. (The Arabic word 'sadaka' means voluntary potential, not obligatory payment of money.)

A summary of orders issued by Muhammad :

- Muhammad cancelled all visits to pagan temples. Muhammad warned the Thakeef tribe and ordered them to destroy the pagan temples Al-Lat and to convert to Islam.

- Muhammad decided to punish his political opponents and the groups who tried to ridicule and kill him. The punishment was death, then having their hearts mutilated.

- Muhammad appointed himself emperor. No one had the right to argue or oppose any of his decisions in any field, either financially, administratively or politically. Any person who refused these regulations would be killed. No one had the right to criticize the distribution of money to Quraish.

- Muhammad decided that all Bedouins should fight in his future military campaigns without any exception, exemption or excuse. One person was to be appointed by Muhammad from his family as a military governor in the capital while Muhammad was fighting outside.

- Muhammad decided on many different punishments for Bedouins who did not participate at all in the campaigns, did not pay money to support the campaigns, or who withdrew from his army.

### The literary style of the Tawba Chapter

As in the whole Quran, Muhammad's style varied throughout each verse, jumping between subjects, repeating them later in different verses, using ambiguous pronouns, using the same pronoun in the plural form to describe all of Muslims, pagan, Christian and Jews and using strange ambiguous words in addressing certain groups. Muhammad also entered stories from Jewish prophets to lengthen the verse and disconnect it from other verses, consequently increasing the ambiguity and complexity.

Muhammad dictated the Quran in a way in which those he addressed directly would understand what he said, but as the message was past on, or reread, it would become increasingly ambiguous and coded (including for Muslims in the next generation). When Othman collated the Quran he also added to this by placing the Tawba chapter in the middle of the Quran and placing the peaceful abrogated Meccan verses at the end of the Quran. This coalition helped the Muslim clergymen in interpreting it however they wanted and in entering many stories and unrelated events to the Tawba chapter, because of the lack of chronological sequence of incidents. Reading any interpretation of those clergymen of the Tawba chapter will put you in the midst of ambiguous, contradictory information. Once they interpreted the battle described as being either Bader Battle or battles with Jews, all battles took place years before the Tawba chapter and had nothing to do with the Tawba chapter. Clergymen aimed to distract the Quran readers' attention from the real truth of this chapter where Muhammad was furious with Muslims. Clergymen changed the name of the chapter from Tawba (redemption) into Saif (sword) saying that this chapter is aimed at Christians and Jews.

In the Tawba chapter, Muhammad mentioned what he said before, that Christians and Jews had to pay high taxes to Muhammad. Clergymen interpreted that Tawba is against Christian and Jews, only to hide Muhammad's cruelty and anger to Muslims. Muhammad did not start this Chapter with classic words in all the Quran in the name of Allah, most benevolent, ever-merciful, as usual, in order to show his anger against Muslims. He wanted to say to Bedouins: this is a message from the emperor of deserts, full of threats, revenge, anger and devoid of mercy, addressed to Muslims and non-Muslims. Muhammad announced his political speech in Tawba by abrogating in total 124 verses and laws in the Quran[50] and all the peaceful Meccan verses.

**Explaining the Tawba Chapter**

I will summarize my interpretation of the Tawba chapter, and omit the lengthy stories from Jewish prophets and the repetitions it contains. Muhammad called Muslims different complex and coded names such as polytheists, tyrannous, fornicators, liars, criminals, losers, dirt and lazy. When he spoke about the punishment of the group of Muslims he referred to them as a sect (Ta'afa in Arabic).

---

[50] Al Nasik and Almansok Pg 139.

**A (declaration) of immunity from Allah and His Messenger, to those of the polytheists with whom ye have contracted mutual alliances.(1)** Muhammad declared that he cancelled his previous treaties with the Muslim Bedouin tribes, and those tribes had to come to Medina to write new agreements. Muhammad used the word polytheist to describe Muslims when they refused to attack other nations. Then he used the same word to describe pagan Bedouins.

**Except the treaties with polytheists who did not deduct anything (4)** Muhammad used an ambiguous term – who did not deduct anything. He is talking about financial payment – when he was talking about the pagan Bedouins who were paying their high taxes (jizya) regularly without any deduction, unlike Muslims who converted into Islam and reduced the amount of money (low tax or zakah) that Muhammad used to receive from them. Muhammad said he was not angry about the pagan Bedouins and their treaties shall not be cancelled, unlike the Muslims. The use of this ambiguous term was to hide the truth from Muslims that Muhammad used to receive high tax from the pagans. Muslim clergymen[51] are very intelligent, here they use the word 'cancel' in interpreting this verse, abusing the similarity in writing in Arabic between the word 'deduction' and 'cancelling', the difference between these two words is one point only in Arabic spelling, accordingly it means that Muhammad was not angry about the polytheist Bedouins, who did not cancel their agreement with Muhammad!

**But when the forbidden months are past, then fight and slay the polytheists wherever you find them (5)** this is Muhammad's decision against all Bedouin Arabs, especially Thakeef, if they did not convert to Islam within four months, they should be killed.

---

[51] Ibn Kathir, pg. 863.

**But if they violate their oaths after their covenant, and taunt you for your Faith, fight ye the chiefs of Unfaith (12)** Muhammad spoke about Muslims who converted to other faiths as an act of heresy when they refused to fight other nations, criticized, objected or argued about Islam or ridiculed Muhammad. Such Muslims shall be punished by death. This legislation constitutes a main part of the Islamic sharia; any reference to Muhammad must be followed by 'peace be upon him', the omission of this phrase is to be punished by death (Muhammad called this punishment 'taan' which, in Arabic, means 'backstabbing'). This meant that his political opponents should be killed. Clergymen referred the term of 'the chiefs of unfaith' to Abu Sufyan, Akrama and other Quraish leaders who died in previous battles years ago in order to distort the history and the truth.

**Fight them, and Allah will punish them by your hands, cover them with shame, help you (to victory) over them, heal the chests of Believers (14)** Muhammad ordered to kill Muslims who opposed him and tried to kill him. In this verse it is obvious that Muhammad was angry with Muslims and wanted revenge.

**Polytheist should not be allowed to build a mosque to Allah (17)** the mosque to Allah is the Dirar Mosque, which Muhammad did not mention explicitly to add his flavour of complexity and coding. Muhammad referred to Muslims in it as infidels, then after a series of long verses, Muhammad turned back to the subject of this mosque. **And there are those who put up a mosque by way of mischief and infidelity, to disunite the Believers (107)**

As we see in this translation, Muslim translators translate the word 'Dirar' to 'mischief' to hide and distort the truth despite the fact it is a noun in Arabic.

Muhammad also mentioned the political opposition and its role in failing the campaign of Tabook. **The foundation of those who so build is never free from suspicion and**

**trembling in their hearts, until their hearts are cut to pieces.** (110) Muhammad did not feel he had had enough from killing Muslims in that mosque for opposing his policy and he wanted to mutilate and cut their hearts to pieces after their deaths[52]. The opponents not only used to meet in this mosque, according to[53] AlJallas bin Sowaid, it used to oppose Muhammad's policies everywhere, he said '*we Muslims are worse than our donkeys, we are a group of naives who are not aware of what surrounds us and want to occupy the whole word with our evils*'.

AlJallas used to spread these words among Muslims. A friend of AlJallas said to him: 'you have spread news and if I mention it, you will be killed, and if I don't report it to Muhammad, I might be killed'. Notice the degree of terror in this man, if he did not inform Muhammad's followers about AlJallas sayings, he might be killed. This is the empire that Muhammad founded on the basis of terror and spies.

Then Muhammad knew about what Aljallas had said, so he summoned him to be interrogated. The political opponents tried to kill Muhammad, but they were unsuccessful, then Muhammad destroyed this opposition by destroying and burning the Dirar Mosque while his opponents were in it. Clergymen fabricated a reason behind destroying the mosque, that a priest called Abu Amer Alraheb was going to pray in the mosque, so Muhammad destroyed it! The other excuse created by clergymen was that the users of the Dirar Mosque used to ridicule a nearby mosque for being a stable, and that for this Muhammad burned their mosque. All these silly excuses are attempts to cover up the cruelty described in the Tabwa chapter.

---

[52] Ibn Kathir, pg. 908 the full list of the presons who build Dirar Mosque and plan to asssacinate Muhammad.
[53] Ibn Kathir Pg 894

**If it be that your fathers, your sons, your brothers, your friends, or your kindred; the wealth that ye have gained; the commerce in which ye fear a decline; or the dwellings in which ye delight - are dearer to you than Allah, Or His Messenger, or the Jihad\* in His cause - then wait until Allah brings about His decision (24)** an obvious and cruel threat to Muslims who did not fight the other nations. He mentioned how Muslims prefer their money, trade, families rather than Muhammad and his wars, so Muhammad said to them wait for punishment. Then he repeated the same word later in a different verse. **We can expect for you either that Allah will send His punishment from Himself, or by our hands. So wait (expectant); we too will wait with you." (52)** Muhammad said to the Muslims 'wait for my cruel and firm response to disobeying my orders'. Saying 'by our hands' means that this punishment will be executed by the hands of Muhammad's faithful followers and Quraish.

**The polytheists are unclean; so let them not, after this year of theirs, approach the Sacred Mosque. And if ye fear poverty, soon will Allah enrich you, (28)** Muhammad describes polytheist as infidels and dirt. 'If ye fear', Muhammad used an ambiguous plural pronoun and each person will explain it in a different way. This speech was addressed to the Quraish who were afraid that their trade

---

\* The real meaning of Jihad in Muhammad's thought, as it is very clear in this verse, is attacking other nations and civilizations with huge armies, enforcing Islam with violence and terror and treating them like slaves, with Arabs as their masters. We have to be very careful with Muslim clergymen, we have to admit they are intelligent in fabrication, they did not use the word 'Jihad', not in the translation, nor in interpretation in this verse, although Muhammad had said it literally in his Quran in this verse because using the word 'Jihad' here obviously clarifies its real meaning. This is why they did not use it here and translate to 'striving in his cause' as a usual ambiguous complicated term. This is why the word Jihad is not fully understood.

might die down when Muhammad banned naked polytheist pilgrimage to the Kaaba. Muhammad assured the Quraish that he would compensate them for this loss with a nice surprise for Quraish. This year is the last year for worshipping of polytheists naked pilgrims. Then Muhammad continues by saying **leave them alone: for they are an abomination (95)** Muhammad angrily here spoke about Muslims who are like dirt, so Muslims and polytheists are dirt.

**The People of the Book, until they pay the Jizya (high tax) with willing submission, and feel themselves subdued (29)** Muhammad repeated his words and previous judgement on Christians and Jews. Clergymen benefited from this repetition to distract attention from the political opposition and trial  to assassinate Muhammad by saying the Tawba addresses only Christians and Jews. Bearing in mind that most of the Quran chapters are full of repetition and mentioning of Christian and Jews. In Tawba there is only one verse where Christians and Jews were mentioned – demanding that they pay high taxes to him.

How Muhammad viewed 'the people of the book'

At first Muhammad tried to connect himself and his religion with Judaism and Christianity by saying that his religion was complimentary to these religions. Muhammad failed to convince Jews to acknowledge him as a prophet, even though his Quran contained a huge number of Jewish stories. When Muhammad failed to persuade the Jews to accept his status as a prophet, he massacred them, murdering their men and capturing their women and children to sell as slaves. He then used this money to buy weapons and horses for his future wars.

Muhammad ordered his successors to exile Jews outside the Arabian Peninsula. This was achieved during Omar bin Alkhattab's reign. Muhammad could exile the Jews because they were scattered tribes in the deserts, unprotected by any international power. Why did Muhammad kill them though, when he could have ordered them to pay a tax instead, as he did with the Christians and as per instructions in verse 29 of the Tawba chapter.

Muhammad considered the Christians (Roman Empire and the Christian villages and tribes) and the Zoroastrians, the fire worshipers (Persian Empire and Zoroastrian Bedouin tribes) as believers and he addressed them with the elegant respectful term 'the people of the Book'. Muhammad treated Zoroastrians and Christians in the same way. He collected high tax (jizya) from both[54]. He did not try to eliminate them in order to avoid interference by the Persian and Roman Empires, as at the beginning of his raids in Medina, they could easily have abolished his small army.

If the Roman Empire had been Jewish, Muhammad would definitely have avoided killing Jews and kept collecting high tax (jizya) from them and instead would have slaughtered Christians.

Muhammad changed this policy when his power and the size of his army increased. Later, he was able to face the Romans and the Persians and fulfil his pledge to fight them, as shown in the Tabook campaign against the Roman Empire by his united army of thirty thousand Bedouin warriors.

The actual understanding of Christians, Jews and Persians (the people of the Book) in the view of Muhammad was in his saying:

*Every infant is born with an instinct and his parents choose either to raise him as Jewish, Christian or Zoroastrian, just like beast brings up beast.* [55]

This is his understanding of these nations and religions, animals begetting other animals. This understanding was transferred to Muhammad's followers. When Almogeerah met the chief of the Persian troops he said: 'those who will

---

[54] Al Bukhari , Aljizya , 3157 and Asbab Al –nizzualm, Al neassbory Pg 212
[55] Sahih Al Bukhari, Al Bukhari, chapter Al Janaz sayings, saying 1359.

survive from our Bedouins troops will enslave you Persians.'

This meant that the Persians would be slaves whether they converted to Islam or not. This proves that the claims of Muslim clergymen about their love and respect to Jesus and other religions were not true. Muhammad, in his speech, compared the followers of other religions to beasts. Those followers were treated like animals, they were forced to pay high tax and lived like second class citizens and slaves for the Bedouin Muslims who destroyed and occupied their civilizations.

Let us complete the interpretation of the Tawba **Go ye forth, (whether equipped) lightly or heavily Go ye forth, (whether equipped) lightly or heavily (41)** these words are metaphoric. What Muhammad meant with 'light weight' was 'young' and with 'heavy' 'old people', so he wanted to call for a war against the neighbouring nations, all Muslims, even the elderly, had to fight. Then Muhammad said **if a contingent from every expedition remained behind, they could devote themselves to studies in religion (122)** this is Muhammad's excuse to keep his family members as military governors from participating in wars. In the Tabook campaign[56] Muhammad kept his cousin, Ali as a military governor in Medina.

**They come to prayer without earnestness; and they offer contributions unwillingly (54)** Muhammad informed Muslims that he knew that their faith, prayers and zakah were superficial, as they were afraid of his sword. He knew that they were paying zakah low tax unwillingly. **And among them are men who slander thee in the matter of (the distribution of) the alms. (58)** Muhammad stressed that no one was allowed to discuss, argue or criticize the issue of financial distribution. He distributed money to

---

[56] Ibn Hisham part 4 pg 173.

Quraish, after the battle of Honain[57]. Once Muhammad distributed the money among others and did not give Abdullah Tamimi the same share [58], Abdullah asked Muhammad to be fair, then Muhammad replied 'if I was not fair who shall be', then Omar said to Muhammad 'shall I kill him?', but Muhammad replied 'no, leave him, he has followers'. So Muhammad had the right to do whatever he wanted without questioning. Omar wanted to kill a Muslim who objected on the unfairness of how Muhammad distributed money, but Muhammad refused to kill him in fear of Abdullah's followers.

**If thou dost question them, they declare (with emphasis); "We were only talking idly and in play." Say: "Was it at Allah, and His Signs, and His Messenger that ye were mocking?" (65)** Muhammad said 'do not dare to ridicule me and my Quran' at the beginning of the Tawba Chapter, Muhammad said that any criticism would lead to the punishment of death and threatened Muslims that he knew what they were saying as he had spies among them[59].

**Make ye no excuses: ye have rejected Faith after ye had accepted it. If we pardon your sect, we will punish other sects, for being criminals (66)** Muhammad refused the Muslims' apologies, saying they meant nothing to him. Muhammad decided that Muslims had to be punished and the punishment would be based on Muhammad's personal decision, which was final. In this verse Muhammad clearly identified the word 'sect' with Muslims who Muhammad decided to punish. Later, Muhammad used this word in other verses in the Tawba chapter. Listeners clearly understood what Muhammad meant when saying sect. - it was the group of Muslims he would punish.

---

[57] Sahih Al Bukhari, Al Bukhari,chapter the wars, Al Magazi sayings 4330 and saying 4331.

[58] Sahih Al Bukhari, Al Bukhari,chapter istitabt al murtadeen, saying 6933.

[59] Ibn Kathir, pg. 890 and also Ibn Hisham part 4 pg 176.

Muhammad used many different punishments, and different forms of torture against Muslims, as he saw fit. He killed and mutilated the hearts of his political opponents and those who planned to kill him. **If, then, Allah brings you back to any sect of them, and they ask thy permission to come out (with thee), say: "Never shall ye come out with me, nor fight an enemy with me: for ye preferred to sit inactive on the first occasion: then sit ye (now) with those who lag behind." (83)** Muhammad had already used the word 'sect' to refer to Muslims he had decided to punish. Muhammad meant by 'Allah bring you back'; the returning of previous eras, eras of attacking Bedouin tribes, so Muhammad attacked and punished the Muslim Bedouin tribes. None of the groups of Muslims who did not participate in the Tabook battle had the right to receive shares of what was taken when Muhammad attacked. Muhammad would decide who would participate in a war and who would benefit from it. As before, Quraish benefited from this again, which compensated its losses from the ban of the naked pagan pilgrims to Mecca.

One of Muhammad's military strategic tactics was to choose a difficult military goal, then some of the Muslim Bedouin tribes would hesitate to participate in his campaign, fearing losses. Immediately afterwards he would then choose an easy military goal, which the Muslims would easily achieve, so that the Bedouin Muslims eagerly participated in the new campaign to gain captives. Muhammad prevented this by banning Muslims who refused to fight in the hard battles from fighting in the easy ones.

In the first campaign that Muhammad carried out against Mecca, the Bedouins hesitated to participate due to the difficulty of this military aim. The campaign ended peacefully through reaching an agreement in the Hudaibia truce. Muhammad then immediately chose an easy military goal, the Jewish tribes of Khaybar. Muhammad banned non-participants in the first battle from enlisting. Muhammad addressed the non-participants in the Mecca campaign by telling them to stay with the people, who stayed in their houses.

Muhammad addressed the non participants in the Tabook campaign as those who lag behind. Muhammad did not differentiate between 'those who stayed at their houses' in the old chapter, replaced by 'those who lag behind' in the Tawba chapter.

The pattern of difficult battle, followed by easy battle was repeated. This and the scorn with which Muhammad showed anyone remaining behind, whatever the reason, was all part of his military and political strategy.

**To the three who were left behind; (they felt guilty) to such a degree that the earth seemed constrained to them, for all its spaciousness (118)** Those three were leaders of Muslim Bedouin tribes who did not join the Tabook campaign [60], they were: Ka'ab bin Malek, Marara bin Rabee' and Hilal bin Omayya Althakafi. Muhammad ordered all Bedouins to boycott those three men for fifty days. No one spoke to them during this time and he ordered their wives to return to their parents' houses. They begged Muhammad until he finally forgave them and he then mentioned them in his Quran, as a lesson to all Muslims. Muhammad also punished other Muslims, for example, ousting Aljad bin Qais from the leadership of the Bani Salma tribe because he did not participate in the war and appointing one of his followers from the tribe as his replacement [61].

The various punishments imposed upon Muslims ranged from destroying their houses and mosques, sending wives to their parents' houses, boycotting anyone from speaking to

---

[60] Sahih Al Bukhari, Al Bukhari,chapter the wars, Al Magazi sayings 4418 and also Ibn Hisham part 4 pg 185.
[61] Ibn Kathir, pg. 885.

them, ousting leaders of tribes and even death. **Let them laugh a little: much will they weep: a recompense for the (evil) that they do (82)** Muhammad threatened Muslims who ridiculed him with cruel punishments. **Nor do thou ever pray for any of them that dies (84)** by this Muhammad said he was no longer afraid of the strong pagan Bedouin tribe leaders. No one would pray over their corpses, even though he himself had prayed, before he was in a position of power, over the corpse of Abdullah bin Salool, the strong pagan tribe leader.

**Nor (is there blame) on those who came to thee to be provided with mounts, and when thou saidst, "I can find no mounts for you," they turned back, their eyes streaming with tears of grief that they had no resources wherewith to provide the expenses (92)** Muhammad spoke about the homeless groups who wanted to fight against the Romans[62], but Muhammad didn't have sufficient money or the means of transport to take them with him. The homeless individuals started to cry, as their only livelihood was through stealing and fighting, then Muhammad reminded the non participating Muslims that they were the main reason behind the failure of the Tabook campaign **Allah hath already informed us of the true state of matters concerning you (94)** after the embarrassment that Muhammad faced by the Kinda tribe when they asked him to guess what they were hiding. He mentioned he did not know the hidden facts as he was a human being and he said that in the Quran, but here Muhammad contradicts that by saying he knew the hidden facts. At his current level of power, who would dare to test him? **We know them: twice shall we punish them: and in addition shall they be sent to a grievous Penalty (101)** Unlike in the rest of the Quran, in Tawba Muhammad aimed at clarity with his threatening speech towards Bedouin, as shown in verse 101. If

---

[62] IIbn Hisham Part 4 Pg 172.

Muhammad said 'we will punish them twice' without completing the verse, the Bedouin should comprehend one punishment while they are alive and the second punishment after death, at the hands of Allah, but Muhammad said those people should be sent to a grievous penalty (hell) so twice punished meant they will suffer this punishment two times in their lives by the faithful followers of Muhammad and Quraish, and then a punishment after death.

Most probably Muhammad attacked, punished and tortured two Muslim tribes, firstly the Judam tribe in a campaign led by Zaid bin Haretha[63] secondly, the Judaima tribe in a campaign led by Khaled bin Waleed[64], so another possibility is that what Muhammad meant by punishment twice was the punishment given to the two Muslim tribes. I say most probably, because all authors of Muhammad's biography mention very clearly that Quraish and Muslims attacked those Muslim tribes before the Tabook campaign and no reason was mentioned for such attacks, although all the details of the attacks were recorded at length - saying these two tribes were Muslims and that they built mosques, before they were attacked and massacred by Muhammad. I do not trust these dates and I think that the attacks took place after the Tabook campaign to punish the Muslims for their disobedience.

We should not forget that Muhammad was consistent in his own vengeful nature and so set vengeful goals against others, even though they embraced Islam and his victories against his enemies. Muhammad killed captives after his victory in the Bader battle, just because one of the war prisoners had spat on Muhammad's face in Mecca many years ago[65] Muhammad also spat on the face of Wahshi three times, when Wahshi became a Muslim asking for

---

[63] Ibn Hisham part 4 pg 268.

[64] Ibn Hisham part 4 pg 77.

[65] Ibn Hisham part 4 pg 22.

forgiveness for killing Muhammad's uncle Hamza in a previous battle, Muhammad never forgave him.

The tribe of Judam years earlier helped the Romans in the Mutta battle against Muhammad in which Muhammad was defeated and his cousin Jaffar was killed, Muhammad cried grievously with bitterness after losing his cousin and he would never forget or forgive the Judam tribe, even after they had become Muslims.

Regarding the attack against the Judaima Tribe, Muhammad chose Khaled bin Waleed to be the leader in this campaign, knowing that the Judaima tribe had killed Khaled's uncle. Muhammad withdrew from this campaign to make it look like a personal aggression from Khaled and to give the appearance that he did not have any responsibility for it. Strangely, Muhammad said that he was innocent from the actions of Khaled bin Waleed, but he did not punish him. Previously, Muhammad insulted Abu Bakr and Omar[66] in his Quran when they only raised their voices in his presence. I open the opportunity for other researchers to study the stories of those attacks, to research and find facts that I have not reached here.

**Take charity from them (103)** Allah ordered a new tax to be imposes Muslims and authorized Muhammad to collect extra money as a form of 'charity' from the Muslim tribes using violence and power. So Zakkah alone was not enough for Muhammad **Know they not that Allah doth accept repentance from His votaries and receives their gifts of charity, (104)** the only way possible for Muhammad to forgive the Muslims was by giving him more money and praising him. The Muslim Bedouin tribes competed among each other in paying the highest tax as a charity to Muhammad, to avoid his anger and punishment that he mentioned in this Chapter. The two Muslim tribes who did not respond to Muhammad's orders received their

---

[66] Quran, sura 49, Al-Hujurat, the Private Apartments, verse 2.

punishments. In this verse when Muhammad said 'Allah', it is obvious that he really meant himself.

## The events after Tawba and Muhammad's threatening speech towards Bedouin Muslims.

efore the Tawba chapter, the Thakeef tribe killed Muhammad's envoy, who was sent to instruct them to stop the religious rituals and pilgrimage and to destroy the temple of Al-Lat. The Thakeef tribe then wanted to renew the contract of praising Al-lat with Muhammad for another three years.

Muhammad refused their proposals because they had killed his envoy. As a result of this refusal and due to the Thakeef awareness of the danger Muhammad and Quraish posed, the Thakeef accepted the conditions of Muhammad and Abu Sufyan. Abu Sufyan, who had at this point lost one of his eyes at the siege of Al-Taf, went along with Almogeerah to destroy the temples and statues of Al-Lat and Minah.

Khaled bin Waleed then went to destroy the temple and statues of Al-Uzza. After this, Muhammad and Abu Sufyan had destroyed all statues and kept Mecca as the only temple destination for pilgrims.

After the emergence of the Tawba chapter, where verses mentioned Muhammad's threats and the obedience of the Thakeef tribe to Muhammad and Quraish by accepting their conditions of destroying Al-Lat and acknowledging the Kaaba as the sole pilgrim destination in the desert, Thakeef was the only tribe Quarish and Muhammad's military coalition could not beat.

After such obedience, the other Bedouin tribes feared the punishment of Muhammad and started peace talks with him, agreeing to pay money and give 'charity' to him. This year was called the year of delegations. Muhammad also started to apply other punishments that he had threatened Muslims with.

Muhammad mentioned names of Muslims whose loyalty was suspicious to him [67] and dismissed them from the mosque in public, explicitly by mentioning their names and saying 'you hypocrites, Get out of here!'

Muhammad's method was copied and became a preferred method used by all Arab kings and presidents when they felt that somebody did not show enough loyalty and enthusiasm towards them, the same dictatorial behaviour, by publicly insulting people and dismissing them from meetings, saying the same words 'you hypocrite, Get out of here'.

---

[67] Ibn Kathir, pg. 904.

# Getting rid of the Satanic Verses

uhammad became Emperor with huge power. He destroyed temples and took control over Al-Taf. He was however concerned about his previous inclusion of what we now call the Satanic Verses, being aware that they would embarrass his followers and Muslim clergymen in the future.

Muhammad would normally have simply abrogated the previous verses where he praised the statues and encouraged Bedouins to visit them – declaring that Allah had changed his mind and the verses were to be deleted. In this case, it is apparent that he did not feel abrogation would be sufficient to explain the enormous contradiction.

The contradiction is indeed massive - in the other verses, Muhammad called for worshipping Allah, without any partner, as this is Islam. In the Satanic Verses, Muhammad declared that Allah had asked for worshipping the other statues. Muhammad therefore had to find a new technique to solve this problem.

Muhammad fabricated a very good story to get rid of these verses, without using the usual abrogation. He created a new story to distract attention of the historical events and its chronological sequence.

Here is the story Muhammad created:

'When he was in Mecca, Jibreel the ghost informed him of the words of Allah which he should speak[68], then the devil took control over Muhammad and completed the verse by saying 'invocation and supplication are the duty of all Muslims'.

The condition of the Thakeef Tribe was mentioned by the devil, so when infidels heard this verse, they were delighted and prayed with Muslims.'

Strangely, in this story, Muhammad said that the infidel masters of Quraish were listening to him. Did they know that Muhammad was going to praise their statues? Muhammad then completed the story by saying:

'In the night following this event, Jibreel the ghost informed Muhammad that those were the words of the devil, not Allah's words[69]. Then Jibreel the ghost informed Muhammad about the new words and decisions of Allah[70] Never did we send a Messenger or a prophet before thee, but, when he framed a desire, Satan threw some (vanity) into his desire.'

Muhammad was intelligent in fabricating his stories. He inserted the events that occurred in medina in old Meccan chapters, but Muhammad forgot to transfer the verse located in the medina chapter where Jibreel the ghost informed him of the new verses. According to Muhammad's claim during the day he was in Mecca with the infidels, while in the night time of the same day he was in medina when Jibreel, being informed about the new verses! It is impossible that

---

[68] Quran, sura 53, An-Najim, the Star, verse 19, this is a Meccan chapter.

[69] Asbab Al nazol –Al neassbory pg 310.

[70] Quran, sura 21, Al–Hajj, the Pilgrimage, verse 52, this is a Medina chapter.

Muhammad was in Mecca during the day and in Medina during the night of the same day, unless he had a Ferrari camel!

I have chosen and interpreted the Tawba chapter as it was the last chapter spoken by Muhammad in his Quran and he passed away shortly after, so he did not have enough time to manipulate its verses.

Muhammad claimed that most of the Quraish masters were sitting and listening to him when he praised their pagan goddesses. Let us see the truth about how Quraish Masters treated Muhammad in Mecca.

One day Muhammad was praying in Mecca, the Masters of Quraish waited until he kneeled down and they threw rubbish, blood, intestines and trash on his head[71] We should also not forget that in the Bader battle, Muhammad killed one of the captives because he spat on Muhammad's face one day in Mecca.

The Quraish Masters in Mecca did not support Muhammad, as he claimed in the story of his own fabrication. How did they treat their shepherd, who claimed prophecy? They threw rubbish at him, spat in his face, called him Abu Kabsha and did not sit with him or listen to him.

---

[71] . Sahih Al Bukhari, chapter jizya saying 3185.

# Extracts from other Chapters

*T*he following pages contain extracts from other Chapters of *Living by the Point of My Spear* and are included here to illustrate some of the other key messages in the book and to elaborate on certain points touched upon in this Chapter.

## The Transforming point of Muhammad's Life

In the early 1600's the Kabaa walls were destroyed by flood[72] and the Quraish rebuilt it. At that time, Muhammad was 35 years old.

After the flood, the Bedouin demolished the ruins of Kabaa and rebuilt it anew. Bedouin tribe leaders fought for five days to be chosen as the tribe leader to place the Black Stone, the most precious stone for Bedouins, on one pillar of Kabaa; whichever tribe placed the stone would gain considerable recognition and respect.

---

[72] Ibn Hisham part 3/ Pg 234

The Bedouin believed in tossing a coin to solve dilemmas, for this reason they decided that the first person to come towards them entering from a certain gate would place the black stone. Coincidentally, it was Muhammad! This ordinary man placed the most precious stone for Bedouins and he was honored by the Bedouin masters.

Muhammad believed a supernatural power had chosen him for this honor, being Ahmassy (from the priest privileged family, Quraish) increased this conviction. The heaven's decision of honoring Muhammad for placing the Black Stone changed his life. Muhammad forgot it was a mere coincidence that might have happened to anyone else who entered this gate in his stead.

## The real motives behind Muhammad's claims of prophecy

The real motives of Muhammad's claims of prophecy were his personal ambition, the desire to gain an acknowledged social status, wealth, the appearance of holiness and the authority that brought within this primitive, cruel society. He also desired to overcome his poverty, which shamed him deeply and did so by marrying a rich, old widow.

When addressing the intellectuals, Muhammad explicitly said that he wanted to unite Bedouin tribes, to be their master, to raid the neighbouring nations, to enslave their men and to use their women to satisfy Bedouin sexual lust.

When Abu Taleb, Muhammad's uncle, fell sick, Quraish masters visited him, chatted about Muhammad's religion and said that Quraish would not attack Muhammad and his followers as long as he agreed to not attack Quraish, her trade and goddesses.

Muhammad responded[73] "if I accept your request, can you give me one word that enables you to control all Arabs and force all foreign nations to believe you and accept you as their lords and masters".

It is obvious that the word to unify Arabs is Islam. Muhammad declared his pure political ambitions under the cover of prophecy, praying, Quran, pilgrimage, etc. These rituals were used as successful methods to control and unify Bedouin tribes under the flag of Quraish, and to attack and control other neighbouring nations.

Al Mothana bin Hareth was a Bedouin Master whose tribe was under the protection of the Persian Empire. Muhammad offered Islam to Al Mothana, but he refused[74], saying that he would not break his agreement with Kisra, the Persian emperor .

Muhammad responded "Be patient, wait and you will see Allah will inherit the Persian's lands and money, furthermore their women will lie down ready for you to rape them - In other words if you, Mothana, embraced Islam, you would own lands, money and women of Persia.

Notice Muhammad's point of view on Persian women. Muhammad imagined that Mothana and Bedouins would be busy all the time raping Persian women.

On another occasion, Muhammad offered Islam to the masters of the Baker Tribe[75], but they refused by saying that they were under the protection of the Persian Empire, who they had a truce with, therefore they did not need Muhammad's religion.

Muhammad said "if you believe in Allah and if Allah decides to keep you alive after the wars, you will enjoy life,

---

[73] Ibn Hisham Part 2/Fg 31

[74] Al Seera Al Nabawiya Al Halabiya Part 2/Pg 4-5

[75] Al Seera Al Nabawiya Al Halabiya Part 2/Pg 5

you will live in  Persians houses, rape Persian women and enslave Persian men.  The true motives of Islam: occupying Iran, stealing Iranian houses and granting them to Bedouins, enslaving Iranian men and raping beautiful Iranian  women.

## Muhammad's treatment of slaves.

*M*uhammad had 24 male slaves and 11 female slaves.

In his Quran, Muhammad discriminated against men according to their colour. He states: "The law of equality is prescribed to you in cases of murder: the free for the free, the slave for the slave, the woman for the woman" [76]. This means that if a white man killed another white man, the killer has to be killed as a punishment for killing a human being, but, if a white man killed a black man, the white man shall not be killed as he did not kill a human being; he has to pay a fine.

Ibn Kathir [77], a scholar in interpreting the Quran, explained this verse saying that the slave is a commodity, and if a slave was killed by mistake or unintentionally, no fine or compensation should be paid. Muhammad also said in his Quran:

"If one (so) kills by mistake a Believer, it is ordained that he should free a believing slave"[78], meaning that if a man killed another man unintentionally, he can erase his sin

[76] Quran 2 The Cow Al Baqarah -178

[77] Ibn kathir Pg 233

[78] Quran , 4the women , An-Nisa 92

by freeing a Muslim slave. Non-Muslim slaves shall not be freed from slavery. If Muhammad aimed to free slaves from their slavery, why did he set this condition? No Jewish or Christian slave shall be freed from slavery!

Muhammad aimed to increase the number of his followers and troops. He saw slaves as commodities and as part of free men's property that can be inherited. The following incident clarifies this:

A dying Muslim man freed 6 of his slaves. After his death, his heirs complained to Muhammad. Muhammad said "If I knew what he did, I would not pray over his corpse!" [79] He felt sorry that he had prayed over a dead Muslim man who had freed his slaves! The story continues … "So Muhammad bought the six slaves and cast lots amongst them, he freed only two slaves and returned the remaining four to the heirs!

Muhammad legitimised ways to return slaves to their slavery and beat them. He said that the master could beat his slave anywhere except his/her face[80], as it might deform them and decrease the value of this commodity! In another verse Muhammad regulated the punishment of an adulterous woman and used discrimination in allocating this punishment, based on the woman's status as master or slave, by saying in his Quran: "If they fall into shame, their punishment is half that for free women" [81]. In a case where the sin of adultery was committed by a slave woman (whether married or single) the punishment should be 50 whips, while the free married woman should be stoned till death [82]. Again Muhammad confirmed that slaves are commodities that shall not be killed, as this will lead to financial losses to their masters.

---

[79] Musnad Al-Imam Ahmed saying number 19158
[80] Sahih Al Bukhari , Al atik saying 2559
[81] Quran , 4the women , An-Nisa 24
[82] Ibn kathir Pg 463

# Muhammad's treatment of women

*M*uhammad's sayings about women are as follows:

[83]"A nation headed by a woman shall never succeed",

[84]"The worst sin and distraction from virtue that I have left for man is woman",

[85]"When I stood on the door of hell, I saw most of its inhabitants were women",

[86] "Women lack brain and religion",

[87] "If I have commanded kneeling for somebody, I would command a woman to kneel for her husband",

[88] "If a man summoned his wife for intercourse and she refused, the angels will curse her till the dawn",

---

[83] Sahih AlBukhari, wars, 4425

[84] Sahih AlBukhari, fornication 5096

[85] Sahih AlBukhari, fornication 5196

[86] Sahih AlBukhari, Menstruation 304

[87] Muhammad's wives, al Sharawy Pg 66

[88] Sahih AlBukhari, fornication 5194

[89] "If a man summoned his wife for intercourse, she has to respond even if she was above the furnace".

"The husband has the right to have sex with his wife even if she is above the camel"

[90] "A woman shall not fast without the permission of her husband"

## Beating of women

In his Quran and Hadith Muhammad legitimised the beating of a wife in the event of any dispute. Violence, beating and physical power become the basis of marital relationships and traditions in the Muslim society for solving any problem.

Muhammad said in his Quran: "As to those women on whose part ye fear disloyalty and ill-conduct, admonish them (first), (next) refuse to share their beds, (and last) beat them; but if they return to obedience, seek not against them means (of further punishment)[91]".

So first the husband has to advise his wife, if she is not convinced, he shall abandon her sexually. If this doesn't work, finally he has the right to punish and beat his wife.

In the last part of the sentence, the fairness of Muhammad is shown by saying "If the wife accepts the husband's conditions, the husband shall stop beating her, because if he continues, this is cruelty". And Muhammad is against cruelty! Muhammad himself had beaten his wife Aisha, hitting her on the chest[92]. Muhammad also said "The man has to hang his whip in a place where the whole family

[89] Marriage and divorce in Islam , Ghassan Ascha Pg54
[90] Sahih AlBukhari, fornication 5192
[91] Quran , 4the women , An-Nisa 34
[92] Marriage and divorce in Islam , Ghassan Ascha Pg 62

can see it" [93] and further, "Man shall not be questioned as to the reason why he beats his family" [94].

Muhammad's orders of Female Circumcisions

Muhammad adopted the Bedouin tradition of cutting away the clitoris by saying that circumcision is an obligation for men, and an honorable deed for women[95]. Muhammad explained the reason behind cutting away the clitoris: a woman may ejaculate before the man!! Why is this a problem? Because it will lead her to conceive a boy with female traits.[96] This is what Bedouins try to avoid for their sons, as the woman is a symbol of weakness for Bedouins, they want their sons to be strong, fierce and violent.

## Forced marriage

One of the most dishonest and unjust legislations of Muhammad against women is that of forced marriage. Muhammad said: "If a man fabricated the acceptance of a woman to marry her by bringing two false witnesses to confirm the marriage, then if the judge confirmed that marriage, although the man and the two witnesses knew that the woman did not accept the marriage herself, the marriage is to be considered legal and valid" [97].

This means that if a man proposed to a woman but she refused to marry him, the man can bring two false witnesses to certify that this woman is his wife, so his marriage shall be considered legitimate and the man has the full right to

---

[93] Marriage and divorce in Islam, Ghassan Ascha Pg 62

[94] Marriage and divorce in Islam, Ghassan Ascha Pg 62

[95] Musnad Al-Imam Ahmed saying number19794

[96] Sahih Al Bukari, prophets sayings 3328 and Sahih Muslim, Menstruation saying 471

[97] Sahih Al Bukhari, Al hee' al, saying 6969,6970,6971

rape this woman as his wife. The woman shall not object to marrying him even if the marriage was fake, she is still forced into it, as this marriage is legalized by Muhammad. This law reflects Muhammad's hatred for women. Any woman can be attained as a legal wife in any way and method, even if it means the use of cheating and forgery.

Muhammad legitimised adultery with a prostitute in his Quran by saying: "Seeing that ye derive benefit from them, give them their money as agreed; but if, after the money is paid, ye agree mutually (to vary it), there is no blame on you"[98]. This means that if a Muslim man admires a woman that is not his wife, he is not considered sinful to entertain himself with her, provided she is willing and he pays her an agreed amount of money. In one saying he has permitted the temporary whoredom.[99]

## Stoning

The Bedouin punishment of adultery was whipping and exiling for one year. As Islam developed out of Bedouin thought and belief, Muhammad legitimised this punishment and quoted it in his Quran:

"The woman and the man guilty of adultery or fornication, flog each of them with a hundred lashes" [100] Muhammad said that the inspiring angel informed him about this punishment.

The first time that Muhammad witnessed the punishment of stoning was when the punishment was being carried out against an adulterous Jewish woman[101]. He was astonished by the punishment and went to Jewish schools to learn more

---

[98] Quran , 4the women , An-Nisa 24

[99] Sahih Al Bukhari, fornication 5116

100 Quran, 24the light , an-nur -2

[101] Sahih Al Bukhari , Quran interpretation saying 4556

about it. Abdullah bin Salam, a former Jew who became a follower of Muhammad accompanied him. The Jews refused to tell him the truth regarding this punishment as they were aware of his intention of quoting all these details in his Quran and claiming it was an inspiration from the angel, so the Jews said they bind adulterous individuals, leave them in the sun and beat them and claimed there was no mention of the stoning punishment in the Torah.

Abdullah bin Salam challenged them by saying: "Liars!" Muhammad started to beg for an answer from the Jews about this punishment, saying "I ask you in the name of God, who gave the Torah to Moses, I ask you in the name of he who rescued the Israelis from the pharaoh's punishment by parting the sea, providing clouds as shade and sent down to you Manna and quail" [102]. Muhammad kept begging until one of the Jews started to read the Torah while hiding the stoning chapter under his hand[103], he read above and underneath his hand without reading this chapter.

Abdullah bin Salam took off the Jewish man's hand saying "What are you hiding here?" The Jew answered "It is the stoning punishment". From that moment Muhammad knew that the punishment of adultery is stoning, but he did not know its details, so Muslims have to refer to the Torah for that. Muhammad said in his Quran: "It was us who revealed the Torah: therein was guidance and light. By its standard have been judged the Jews, by the Prophets who bowed (as in Islam) to Allah's Will"[104].

Furthermore Muhammad said: "My decisions and judgments are based on what is written in the Torah" [105]. Due to Jewish refusal, Muhammad did not quote the stoning punishment in his Quran. Muhammad practiced by himself

---

[102] Ibn Kathir Pg 619 -620

[103] Sahih Al Bukhari , Quran interpretation saying 4556

[104] Quran ,5 the feast, Al –Maidah-44

[105] Asbabb Al Nuzzul , Al Neassbcry Pg 197

the brutal and cruel punishment of stoning and legitimised it in Islam[106]. The Muslim clergymen are now confused about the legitimisation of this punishment, as there is no quote in the Quran.

Muhammad despised women and discriminated against them even in the punishment of adultery. The adulterous man stands in the middle of a yard surrounded by Muslims who stone him. If he is lucky and the first stones are not fatal, he can run and escape. His punishment is complete and if he survives, it is considered as Allah's will to rescue him. On the contrary, the adulterous woman shall be placed in a large hole and buried to the line of her shoulders, this hole shall be in the middle of a yard, surrounded by Muslims who stone her, but the woman can not escape, so Muhammad can ensure her death.

Muhammad claimed that the inspiring angle – the ghost – used to visit him several times a day and informed him of everything going on around, like conspiracies for his assassination, especially if plotted by Jews, such as Bani Natheer's clan.

If this is the case, why did Muhammad beg for an answer from the Jews about the punishment of adultery? Why do we have to read the Torah to apply this punishment? And why did Allah send Muhammad and his Quran if we have to follow the Torah?

---

[106] Sahih Al Bukhari , Al Muharben saying number 6830

## Terrorism and brutality in Muhammad's thoughts and actions

*U*m Kirfa (Fatima bint Rabeea bin Bader AlFazarri) was a woman who became the governor of her tribe and a symbol of pride, social status and respect. We know this as more than 50 swords hung in her house, which she had received as gifts from other tribe leaders, she also had twelve sons[107].

Regrettably, Muhammad's followers attacked her tribe by hiding through the day and creeping during the night[108]. Um Kirfa and her beautiful daughter were captured by Muhammad's followers.

Muslims were against the idea of a woman governing a tribe, as Muhammad had said "A nation headed by a woman shall never succeed" so they tortured her alive by tying her legs to two different camels running in two different directions, tearing Um Kirfa into two halves. They

---

[107] Al Seera Al Nabawiya Al Halabiya Part3 / Pg 180

[108] Al Seera Al Nabawiya Al Halabiya Part3 / Pg 174 Ibn Hisham Part 4/pg 273 and systematic reading in Islam by Dr Al Najar Pg 58

then chopped up her body and presented her head as a gift to Muhammad in Medina.

Muhammad ordered that Um Kirfa's head be shown throughout the streets of Medina to teach people a good lesson. Muhammad gave his uncle, Hoozan bin Abi Wahab, the daughter of Um Kirfa to entertain himself.

When Muhammad occupied Khaybar, he thought that Kinanah bin Rabee owned the treasures of Bani Natheer's clan, so he threatened him with death if he did not tell them the location of the treasure [109]. One of Muhammad's followers said that Kinanah used to visit a certain spot of land, so the Muslims digged at this location, but without success. Muhammad therefore ordered his fellow Zabeer bin Awwam to torture Kinanah until he confessed. He burned Kinanah's chest and body until he fell unconscious. When Kinanah woke up, Muhammad ordered another follower called Muhammad Bin Mosalamh to torture Kinanah and eventually behead him.

Another story involved a poor follower of Muhammad's in Medina whose wealth was only a Christian slave. Muhammad helped him by auctioning the Christian slave himself to increase his price and encourage higher bids[110]. Naeem bin Naham bought the slave for 800 dirham. This indicates that when the Sudanese sell Christians as their slaves, they apply regulations of their religion and do the same as their messenger.

## Muhammad's racism against the Turks

Muhammad despised and hated Persia, the closest empire to Bedouins. Moreover, Muhammad described

[109] Ibn Hisam part 3 / Pg 366

[110] Sahih Al Bukhari, al Akrah saying number 6947

Turks by saying to his Bedouins followers" Before the end
of the world, you shall fight Turks, whose eyes are small
and noses flattened and who have ugly reddish faces, like
hammered shields" [111] . His description of Turks was
degrading and aggressive and reflected Muhammad's point
of view of other nations. The only nation Muhammad had
respect for was his own. He saw the men of other nations as
enemies, or commodities to be enslaved.

## Muhammad was a Murderer

When Muhammad said "Living by the point of my
spear" he meant it literally and he lived by the point of his
spear.

Muhammad killed Abi Bin Khalaf Bin Wahab by
stabbing him with his spear[112].

Bin Wahab years ago[113] smacked Muhammad in the
face, Muhammad never forgot that and Muhammad
murdered him to gain personal revenge, furthermore, this
was not the first human killed by the hands of the prophet.
Muhammad also killed Amro Bin Umer[114] with his sword;
when he went back home, he gave his sword to his
daughter, Fatima[115], to wash off the human blood.

The truth has been hidden for 1,400 years - Muhammad is a
murderer

---

[111] Sahih Al Bukhari , jihad and biography saying number 2928 and 2927
[112] Ibn Hisham part 3 pg 90& p143 , Al Seera Al Nabawuya (Al Halabiya)
Khaffaji Al Halabi, part 2 pg 237
[113] Sirat Rasul (Ibn Ishaq) compile Mohammed hammed Allah , p 125.
[114] Ibid
[115] Ibn Hisham part 3 pg 111.